Thinking Like a Teacher

Thinking Like a Teacher

Preparing New Teachers for Today's Classrooms

Foreword by Janet Alsup

Jo-Anne Kerr and Linda Norris

ROWMAN & LITTLEFIELD
Lanham • Boulder • New York • London

Published by Rowman & Littlefield
A wholly owned subsidiary of The Rowman & Littlefield Publishing Group, Inc.
4501 Forbes Boulevard, Suite 200, Lanham, Maryland 20706
www.rowman.com

Unit A, Whitacre Mews, 26-34 Stannary Street, London SE11 4AB

British Library Cataloguing in Publication Information Available

Library of Congress Cataloging-in-Publication Data

978-1-4758-3372-0 (cloth : alk. paper)
978-1-4758-3373-7 (pbk. : alk. paper)
978-1-4758-3374-4 (electronic)

♾™ The paper used in this publication meets the minimum requirements of American National Standard for Information Sciences—Permanence of Paper for Printed Library Materials, ANSI/NISO Z39.48-1992.

Printed in the United States of America

To all new teachers and their mentors who inspire them to think like teachers.
And to our parents and grandparents, our first teachers.

Thought flows in terms of stories—stories about events, stories about people, and stories about intentions and achievements. The best teachers are the best storytellers. We learn in the form of stories.

—Frank Smith *To Think*, Teachers College Press, 1990

Contents

Foreword

Janet Alsup

Throughout my career as an English teacher educator, I struggled with how to make the methods classroom seem "real," when I knew it really wasn't—how to make university-based instruction about teaching simulate real-world classrooms full of real-life adolescents. In order to make the methods experience more practical, I often asked students to "micro-teach" lessons to their peers, watch videos of others teaching and critique them, or write reflective journals about their own observations of practicing teachers in schools. However, too often these same pre-service teachers ended their coursework with a feeling of infallibility, a sense of readiness to teach if only they would be released to do it. While I appreciated the confidence, such an attitude often predicted a hard fall when the teacher candidate finally assumed his or her first classroom, and a sense of dismay and frustration resulted. Their best laid plans did not seem to work as intended; they were not as prepared and skilled as they imagined. The everyday challenges of a teaching life intruded on their earlier confidence, on their careful university methods course instruction, and the new teachers felt that they had to choose between enacting what the university taught and what the real-world seemed to demand, what their professors told them constituted good teaching and what they believed they must do to survive. Consequently, many of these young teachers reverted to teaching as they were taught, not as they were taught to teach.

How do we as teacher educators better help teacher candidates to transition from student, to student teacher, and, finally, to teacher? How do we help them effectively integrate what they learn at the university with what they see in their internships and first years of teaching? How do we help teacher candidates experience, and engage in, what I have called "borderland discourse" (Alsup, 2006)? I define borderland discourse as language that reflects "an enhanced consciousness, a meta-awareness of thought and action that can

ix

incorporate the personal as well as the professional, and multifaceted, contextual, and sometimes contradictory ideologies and situated identities" (p. 125). When a young teacher engages in such complex discourses that straddle personal and professional expectations and exigencies, her professional identity expands to encapsulate both her own subjective preferences and perceived school and societal demands. Ideally, such identity growth results in the development of a more complete, and satisfying sense of teacher self. The problem is that borderland discourse doesn't always happen on its own, and it depends on effective mentorship, usually during the student teaching internship or early field practica. How might we encourage borderland discourses earlier, during the methods courses prior to student teaching?

Linda Norris and Jo-Anne Kerr have assembled a book that might just provide a solution. Their text can help teacher candidates access borderland discourse more efficiently and earlier in their educational careers. Theirs is a brilliant approach to guiding young teachers toward a more integrated and satisfying professional identity—an identity that could mark the beginning of a sustainable teaching career. So how do they do this? Norris and Kerr share stories told by teacher candidates themselves to prompt critical reflection and identity growth on the part of readers.

The book you are about the read incorporates fifteen narratives from new English teachers fresh to the classroom out of the university; these narratives are responded to both by the new teachers themselves and their former teacher educators, Norris and Kerr. Finally, discussion questions are included that help the readers, presumably teacher candidates or new teachers themselves, engage in a parallel, if vicarious, kind of narrative borderland discourse through reading. And all of this happens within the framework for teaching outlined in Charlotte Danielson's 2007 book, *Enhancing Professional Practice: A Framework for Teaching.* So the young teachers are storytelling, but storytelling within a frame, a frame encouraging focused critical reflection. The stories themselves are examples of borderland discourse in action, as teacher candidates re-tell their experiences and nearly simultaneously examine and express how these experiences might be understood through a professional, more distanced and research-based, lens. The stories and consequent reflections on the stories become borderland discourse.

How does a narrative simulate an experience, such as teaching? Empathy can be defined as an expression of emotion in response to witnessing another's emotional state; it is an affective response to another's situation largely consisting of imagining the feelings of the other. It follows that narrative empathy is empathy experienced when reading or hearing a story, a story that may be truth or fiction. The empathy is vicariously experienced through mediation with printed or oral language. The words of the narrative produce imagined scenarios during which the listener or reader identifies with characters or authors, and in this way lives through a simulated experience without any real-world effects. Such vicarious or simulated narrative experience can be a wonderful way to think through issues, problems, or hypothetical challenges—before confronting them in real life. The stories in *Thinking Like a Teacher* offer up narrative classroom worlds, and sample responses to them, that the pre-service teacher reader can experience vicariously—as simulations of a future, real-world classroom. In this way the reader can explore options and possibilities, and even discuss them with peers and teachers, prior to experiencing them in any high stakes setting. Norris and Kerr spend some time in their book explaining the power of storytelling and story-hearing before relating such narrative theories to teacher education. And after reading their text, I can see the application of this theory very clearly. Teachers tell stories, other teachers listen, respond, and project into their own possible professional futures. Through narrative experience, and narrative empathy, such pre-service teacher readers can respond to and engage in the borderland discourse of identity development.

Teachers' stories as told in this book are expressions of communities of practice and can be simulated contexts for teacher identity growth. *Thinking Like a Teacher* can help young teachers who read it work through problems they will surely face and that are faced by the teacher-storytellers in the book: classroom management, time management, differentiation, classroom culture, assessment, and responding to authority, among others. The book might also serve as a model of how storytelling itself can be a pivotal and empowering tool in the teacher toolbox as teachers move from novice to experienced. Storytelling can be used throughout a career, as a way to share, gain, and reflect on knowledge, as different challenges arise.

In the end, *Thinking Like a Teacher* is a collection of reflective teacher stories, a readable book discussing theories of teaching and learning to be a teacher, as well as a textbook prompting teacher candidates and their instructors to have critical conversations about teacher identity development. Learning to be a teacher is an incredibly complex, challenging process. There are many issues to be addressed and confronted. This book both argues, and enacts, the premise that telling stories is a key part of effective teacher education. In essence, Kerr and Norris operationalize storytelling for teacher education and provide a pathway to make those methods courses more real, make them more honest simulations of actual teaching experience, which will surely help young teachers thrive.

REFERENCES

Alsup, J. (2006). *Teacher identity discourses: Negotiating personal and professional spaces.* New York: Routledge.

Danielson, C. (2007). *Enhancing professional practice: A Framework for teaching.* Alexandria, VA: Association for Supervision and Curriculum Development.

Preface

Sarah Rhodes

In this preface, Sara recounts an incident early in her experience as a teacher that demonstrates how unpredictable events combined with adolescent behavior can quickly derail careful planning and preparation. Sara also shares with readers how her experience and the resulting frustration led to this collection of teacher narratives, a collection designed to help preservice and novice practitioners learn to think more deliberately like experienced teachers.

It seems only fitting that the idea for this book grew from my telling Dr. Jo-Anne Kerr a story. Well, telling is not exactly the right word. I was venting. "I was so frustrated!" I said while in her office one day in May 2013. I had just completed a seven-week substitute teaching assignment with a group of energetic seventh graders. I had been tasked with teaching them how to conduct, write, and present research. This was the first time that they had completed a research project.

We started in the library, learning how to locate sources, how to take notes, and how to cite sources. We worked on creating logical outlines, discussing how they could be used as a planning tool to help us in our writing and speaking. We worked together, writing researched essays on Greek mythological figures, practicing our public speaking skills for a class presentation, and learning what makes an effective visual aid for a presentation. It was a unit that I worked hard to facilitate with the materials left for me by their classroom teacher. And it seemed to be going fairly well. That is, until the day before the papers were due.

My first period class and I walked from my classroom to the computer lab across the hall. I was very fortunate; my classroom was near the library and computers labs, so the trip did not take up too much class time. Students were going to finish typing final drafts of their papers. However, when we arrived in the lab, we discovered that half of the laptops were not charged, as a previous class of students had not plugged them in.

While I was trying to handle this unforeseen situation, one-quarter of my students were working. What about the other three-quarters? They were standing right next to me, either a) insisting on an urgent need for the restroom; b) asking to go to their lockers to fetch their pencils, pens, research folders, etc.; or c) asking me yet again for another copy of the rubric or assignment checklist. And while I was trying to deal with all of this, the guidance counselor came in with a new student. (I had no idea that a new student would be joining the class.)

At that moment, I had never more wanted a pause button. The research project that I was implementing was a seventh grade curricular requirement; I couldn't exempt the new student from it. But it was due the next day! How was I going to accommodate him in addition to making him feel welcome in my English language arts classroom? What was I going to do with the students who were clamoring to use the restroom? Go to their lockers? How and when were my students going to finish typing their papers, given that half of the laptops were not working? In my teacher education courses, I had been introduced to Charlotte Danielson's *Framework for Teaching* (2007) and her "Four Domains of Teaching Responsibly: Planning and Preparation, The Classroom Environment, Instruction, and Professional Responsibilities." Danielson's domains accurately capture what veteran teachers have known for years—instruction is only one-quarter of what teachers have to manage. Yes, we must plan and prepare instruction; however, this planning must also account for the vagaries of the classroom environment, those unanticipated events (such as uncharged laptops and the arrival of a new student in the middle of a unit).

In light of the realities of today's learning environments, Domain 2: Classroom Environment includes not only the creation and maintenance of a welcoming and secure place in which our students can learn but must also function as a well-organized, well-oiled machine that helps the teacher deal with the numerous intricacies and unpredictable events that steal time from instruction. Domain 4: Professionalism also comes into play, as we advocate for our students and provide service to them while simultaneously modeling how to handle the often chaotic world of teaching and learning with grace, dignity, poise, and patience.

A key challenge of teaching, often not acknowledged, is adhering to best practice strategies and instruction despite the vagaries that occur almost on a day-to-day basis. Teachers are allotted a number of days of instruction, yet they are also faced with the prospect of instructional time being cut short due to a wide range of unanticipated events, from weather delays to early dismissals to assemblies to power outages. A period cut short by twenty minutes because of a weather delay or an unexpected early dismissal can certainly have an adverse effect on one's careful planning and implementation of best practice. And the fabulous interactive PowerPoint presentation that I spent hours creating couldn't be used as I had planned because of a power outage.

It was this aspect of teaching, preparing for and managing the unknown, that got Dr. Kerr and me thinking about how teacher preparation programs can better prepare their preservice teachers for the realities of teaching and of today's learning environments.

First, we reached out to Dr. Linda Norris, a colleague of Dr. Kerr's and former professor of mine. We thought we could collaborate on an article about this topic for a professional journal. Then Dr. Kerr and Dr. Norris received the 2014 National Council of Teachers of English (NCTE) annual convention call for proposals. The theme for the convention, "Story as a Landscape of Knowing," could be reflected, we believed, if we highlighted my story as capturing this mostly overlooked facet of teaching.

We dove into preparation, planning to use my story, along with a theoretical framework concerning teacher identity and the development of professional dispositions, to offer a panel discussion that would focus on how teacher educators can help preservice teachers prepare for what CEE (the Conference on English Education) calls "the vagaries of the learning environment."

Our proposal was accepted, and we began to plan our panel. A few weeks prior to the convention, Dr. Kerr received an e-mail from an acquisitions editor at Rowman & Littlefield Publishers. Having seen our panel listed on the convention program on the NCTE website, she was interested in meeting with us at the convention to discuss the possibility of developing a book on this topic. While attending the convention, we met with the editor and were invited to write and submit a prospective. A few months later, we were offered a contract.

This endeavor has evolved beyond my wildest dreams, and I am grateful for the opportunity to contribute to a work that will, I believe, help teacher candidates learn how to think like a teacher so that they will be able to gracefully and effectively handle the challenges of teaching.

REFERENCE

Danielson, C. (2007). *Enhancing professional practice: A Framework for teaching.* 2nd ed. Alexandria, VA: Association for Supervision and Curriculum Development.

Acknowledgments

We thank the fifteen dedicated teachers who courageously shared truths about what happened in their early days of teaching. Nothing has been fabricated. They were all willing to write about and to discuss with us what they experienced so that other new teachers could benefit from their stories. What a generous gift. It was both memorable and enriching to read our contributors' stories, to listen to them, and to talk with everyone who contributed to this project and to witness the growth and development of our graduates as they began their careers. We hope we will all keep in touch and continue to learn from and with one another.

We owe a large debt of gratitude to the cooperating teachers who have mentored our teacher candidates over many years; we have witnessed first-hand how they have taught and modeled for our beginners what it means to be a professional.

We so appreciate our reviewers, Rick Beach, Brad Minnick, Roxanne Rouse, and Helen (Nan) Sitler, who took time and care to read our manuscript, offer expert suggestions, and write such lovely endorsements. And we are ever grateful for the willingness of our generous colleague, Janet Alsup, to write such a thought-provoking and meaningful Foreword.

Heartfelt thanks to Sara Rhodes, whose story was the catalyst for this project and who offered valuable information and assistance that encouraged this publication to fruition, and who suggested adding her cooperating teacher's checklist. We thank her for her willingness not only to share some of the challenges she faced but also to collaborate with us to devise ways to improve our teacher education program.

Thank you to former Rowman & Littlefield acquisitions editor Susanne Canavan for reaching out to us and encouraging us to share our NCTE panel presentation with this wider audience, and to our current editors at Rowman

& Littlefield, especially Tom Koerner, for the thoughtful and supportive feedback that they offered throughout the process of writing and organizing this collection. And special thanks to attorney Richard Flickinger for helping us understand the language of a book contract.

Linda thanks her family, Bob, KJ, and Kimberly, who support all of her work, pray for her, and provide love and encouragement. Jo-Anne extends gratitude to her supportive and ever-patient husband, Larry.

Introduction

Linda Norris and Jo-Anne Kerr

The purpose of this book is to assist new teachers and teacher educators in identifying and exploring issues and problems new teachers confront every day; it is a collection of fifteen novice teacher stories with reflective analyses followed by commentary, questions, and suggested readings from us, Jo-Anne and Linda, two former secondary English teachers and current teacher educators with a combined thirty-five years of university methods course and supervisory field experience.

We situate these new teacher narratives in a well-recognized framework for teaching. Our hope is to provide preservice teachers in methods classes and teachers early in their practice with greater awareness of how to think like expert teachers and how to come to terms with surprising, difficult, or unplanned situations.

We aim to help new teachers navigate the rough waters of the early years by offering specific ways to strategize like an expert teacher through actual situations and challenges faced by graduates of our English Education program at Indiana University of Pennsylvania, one of the largest of the fourteen state-system universities in Pennsylvania, where we have been training teachers for the past twenty-four years.

This collection has three key purposes: (1) to highlight the challenges that new teachers face when they are confronted by unanticipated events and circumstances that affect implementation of best practice; (2) to provide opportunity for preservice teachers to become cognizant of day-to-day realities of the classroom and to consider how these realities may affect their pedagogy through a framework of best practice; and (3) to help pre-service teachers begin the construction of a professional identity that includes the ability to think like a more experienced teacher and thus to continue to grow professionally.

New teachers often leave the field within the first three years of teaching; some of the top reasons are "salary, student behavior, lack of support, and too much testing" (Fioriello, 2015). This text contributes to understandings of how to retain and to sustain new teachers by offering situations with which preservice and novice teachers can identify and by providing strategies to cope with daily concerns and dilemmas they face in the schools, from minor distractions, including students coming in late for class, to major issues, such as violent behavior (see, for example, McCarthy & Norris, 2013).

Discussing the narratives in *Thinking Like a Teacher* in methods courses and during field experiences, and writing and reflecting about their own pre-student teaching and student teaching experiences, will help teacher candidates understand their shift in role from student to teacher, a goal articulated by the Conference on English Education in "What Do We Know and Believe about the Roles of Methods Courses and Field Experiences in English Education?" (2005): "Teacher candidates need to become explicitly aware of teachers' instructional choices, student needs and behavior, and the vagaries of the learning environment in a way which points them toward their new role as instructional leaders rather than instructional consumers" (p. 6).

This text introduces what Linda Norris refers to as "situational pedagogy," meaning that in any given classroom situation or teaching moment, there are always multiple choices available and spontaneous decisions teachers have to make that may help or hinder the outcome of that moment in space and time (see also Kerr & Norris, 2008, 2010; Miller & Norris, 2007). The novice teacher narratives included here provide several instances of situational pedagogy and the choices and decisions these teachers, early in their practice, made when faced with daily predicaments.

These scenarios encourage discussion about the best or most expert pedagogical practices new teachers could make and/or might consider in those or similar situations. Our goal is that by sharing the choices these new teachers made, and by noticing and discussing their circumstances, other new teachers can learn and benefit when confronted with similar circumstances and can therefore apply more expertise earlier in their practice.

Just as editors Mahiri and Freedman's research (2014) assists new teachers to become more acutely aware of factors that they can "control as a teacher (classroom setup, curriculum, student expectations, and teacher-student dialogue)" through the "teacher as learner" concept (p. 186), our book also advocates the use of metacognitive processes in situational pedagogy that teachers in their early experiences should continue to hone in future years.

A NEED FOR ADAPTIVE EXPERTISE

Our collection has its genesis in a story, a story shared by Sara Rhodes, a secondary English teacher graduate from our program in 2011. Sara's story demonstrates a truth about teaching not often acknowledged in teacher preparation programs. Indeed, the "best laid plans" do often "go awry" in the world of teaching.

Teacher candidates learn how to plan lessons that are pedagogically sound in their methods courses. They become knowledgeable about learner development in their educational psychology courses. They become familiar with strategies for working with diverse learners. However, they are often not taught and do not necessarily know what to do and how to cope when the realities of day-to-day teaching interfere, in sometimes devastating ways, with their careful planning and even with the understandings about teaching and learning that they have amassed in the four short years they spend developing their expertise and teaching personas.

Linda Darling-Hammond (2006) makes the case that teachers must become "Adaptive Experts" and states, "Modern learning theory implies that teachers must be diagnosticians, knowledge organizers, and skilled coaches to help students master complex information and skills. Thus, the desire to succeed at much more formidable learning goals with a much more varied student population radically changes the nature of teaching and the challenges of teacher preparation" (p. 10).

Darling-Hammond adds, "If teachers are to help learners who begin and proceed differently reach similar outcomes, they will need to engage in disciplined experimentation, incisive interpretation of complex events, and rigorous reflection to adjust their teaching based on student outcomes" (p.11). Through this characterization of teaching, it is clear that teaching is a complex endeavor, one that necessitates juggling multiple roles and modes of thinking, oftentimes at a lightning pace.

Thinking Like a Teacher is grounded in theory that suggests the centrality of story in our lives as a way of rendering thought, the concept of dispositional intelligence, and in scholarship that examines the construction of a teaching identity. An examination of this scholarship will be followed by an overview of the narratives in this collection, each of which includes commentary, analyses, and questions that invite reflection on the challenges that today's learning environments present to new teachers, teachers who, while having to take responsibility for educating others, are nonetheless not fully self-actualized professionals themselves.

NARRATIVE AS A MODE OF THOUGHT

The argument that we use narrative (story) thinking was put forth first by Jerome Bruner and later was applied to education and research methodology by others. In *Actual Minds, Possible Worlds* (1986), Bruner identifies what he calls "two modes of thought" (p. 11), one of which he labels "paradigmatic" and the other "narrative" (pp. 12–13), both of which entail their own ways of rendering experience. Peter Smagorinsky (2008) offers a summary of Bruner's theory, pointing out that the paradigmatic mode is the "most widely emphasized way of knowing in American schools" (p. 12).

Trimmer (1997) alludes to this same privileging of the paradigmatic mode of thinking in research and scholarship about teaching. He writes that while teachers love to tell stories about teaching, the profession does not "trust" these stories, as they are neither reliable nor verifiable (pp. x–xi). Instead, the creation of knowledge about teaching must follow criteria for empirical or ethnographic research. If stories are used, they are relegated to introductions or anecdotes (p. xi).

However, Trimmer sees stories as a means to "explore different ways to report information on teaching and learning" (p. xii), thus making a case for the ability of these stories to present a "truth" about teaching that may be obscured by the "sanctioned procedures of educational research" (p. xii). Britzman (2003) likewise asserts the value and validity of viewing teachers (and their voices and stories) as sources of knowledge. For Britzman, such research methodology privileges the "voices of those experiencing educational life," thus maintaining that these voices are indeed sources of knowledge (p. 66).

OPPORTUNITIES TO
ENGAGE IN REFLECTION AND INTERPRETATION

When we ask novice teachers to revisit their narratives and when our readers engage with these narratives, they, much like novice readers, enter into what Sheridan Blau (2003) calls "authentic reflection and interpretation" (p. 22). Reflection and interpretation often begin with what Blau and Dewey (1910) term a necessary and healthy "confusion" in order to reach higher levels of understanding, analyzing, and evaluating a particular situation to make better meaning of it.

When new teachers regularly engage in making meaning of a situation, in analyzing the component parts by reconstructing the scenario, and in judging the strong and weak points of their choices at the time, they become equipped with critical skills they will need to use in future situations. We contend that as our readers engage with the narratives we share, they will construct deeper understandings about day-to-day teaching through their own interpretations of and reflections on the stories.

DISPOSITIONS AND DISPOSITIONAL INTELLIGENCE

For preservice teachers, knowledge and skills in and of themselves are insufficient if they are not augmented by practice in ways of thinking (dispositions) about teaching, in our case, dispositions that concern the complexities of the learning environment and how to manage these successfully. Our teacher stories provide insights into teaching realities and prompting to think more deeply about these realities, thus promoting the development of dispositional intelligence—a way of thinking about teaching that includes knowledge and skills and also a predisposition to use pedagogical knowledge in ways that situations demand.

This understanding of pedagogical knowledge dependent upon the situated realities of the learning environment will also allow for the development of what we referred to earlier from Linda Darling-Hammond as "adaptive expertise" and what Linda Norris terms "situational pedagogy," necessary skills for successful teaching.

Schussler (2006) asserts that dispositions "are at the root of teachers' decisions to think and act" (p. 252), documenting a rise of interest in dispositions and exploring how education programs can foster the development of dispositions in teacher candidates. Katz and Raths (1985) also apply dispositions to teacher education, defining them as acts that appear spontaneous but are, in fact, deliberate, conscious, and attentive to what is occurring in the context of actions. And the Interstate Teacher Assessment and Support Consortium recognizes that appropriate dispositions are key to effective teaching, defining critical dispositions as "habits of professional action and moral commitments" (Council of Chief State Officers, 2012, p. 6).

For dispositions and dispositional intelligence to develop, there must be an "immersion in contexts that nurture the desired disposition in complex ways" (Brent, 2012, p. 563). Tishman, Jay and Perkins (1993) characterize this immersion as "enculturation" (p. 8) that takes place in a "sustained cultural context" comprised of "exemplars, cultural interaction, and direct instruction" (p. 9). Our teacher narratives are exemplars in which our readers can immerse themselves. And the accompanying commentary, questions, and invitations to reflect provide a means by which readers can engage in interaction with guidance offered by instructors.

EVIDENTIARY REASONING AND REFLECTIVE PRACTICE

Blau's (2003) notion of *"evidentiary reasoning* that is the basis for effective intellectual work in any academic field or profession . . . and that also defines critical thinking in every enterprise of business, civic, or private life" (p. 53; emphasis added) comes into play when our readers respond to questions about the narratives and then reexamine the narratives for evidence to support and augment their responses. Using evidentiary reasoning will provide practice with this type of intellectual activity, an activity that, it is hoped, will eventually become a habit of mind—a disposition. While opportunity for evidentiary reasoning will be offered in each chapter, opportunity for reflection, another key disposition, is likewise offered.

Kathleen Blake Yancey in *Teaching Literature as Reflective Practice* (2004) credits Dewey that reflection is "habitual and learned" (p. 13). She goes on to explain that reflection is also a Vygotskian concept as an "activity of consciousness" and that reflection is a combination of both formal learned concepts and spontaneous, situational concepts: "Reflection, however, requires both kinds of thinking, the scientific and the spontaneous, the strength of scientific concepts deriving from their 'conscious and deliberate character,' and the spontaneous from 'the situational, empirical, and practical'" (from *Thought and Language*, p. 194, cited in Yancey, p. 13).

Yancey builds on this epistemology by adding Donald Schon's perspective from his work, "Causality," that there are two kinds of reflection: "Reflection-in-action is the process of thinking about the nature of a practice while that practice is ongoing. Reflective transfer is the process of thinking that allows us to generalize from specifics, to develop schemata and other models that move us from one specific instance to another, and to create a prototype that lends itself to transfer (see Schon, "Causality," in Yancey, pp. 50–51 and Schon in Goodman & Fisher, pp. 69–102).

Our book's narratives illustrate beginning teachers' "readings" of situations, their "reading" responses, and their conscious reflection-in-action on their specific teaching and learning situations. Our new teacher narratives also demonstrate reflective transfer, allowing them and other new teachers who read their stories to create what McCutcheon (1992) calls a "theory of action" that can be applied when and if a similar situation arises.

Much like novice readers who become capable of reading more difficult texts as they learn what to do as readers and then generalize those skills in reading new texts, our novice teachers become more capable "readers" of their learning environments, developing the requisite coping skills that can then be applied when needed, the adaptive expertise that Darling-Hammond states that effective teachers must enact.

These same practices advocated by experts in the English language arts and that foster the development of reflective thinking are exactly the dispositions we desire to engender in teacher candidates. Yancey (2004) states, "Through reflection and awareness, a reader is developed" (p. 15); we would assert that through reflection and awareness, an expert teacher is also developed.

TEACHER IDENTITY CONSTRUCTION

Of particular relevance to this collection is the construction of a professional identity for both preservice and novice teachers, construction that is fraught with complexities, challenges, and threats. Janet Alsup (2006) reminds us that, "being a successful secondary teacher is much more complex than is normally recognized or shared with teacher education students" (p. xiii). Britzman (2003) makes the case that being a teacher mixes the personal and the professional, writing of her experience as a teacher candidate: "it dawned upon me that learning to teach was doing something to who I was becoming" (p. 12). And with reference to student teachers, she points out the problem with "the identity of the teacher as expert," given that student teachers are being educated themselves as they are educating others (p. 228).

Alsup (2006) contends that teacher education programs tend to ignore "the development of the teacher him- or herself," focusing instead on the preservice teacher's future students (p. xiv). Yet Miller and Norris (2007) point out the difficulties inherent within this process, stating that the preservice teacher identity is "vulnerable to being co-constructed by competing agendas" at the same time as it is "predetermined because of institutional and social expectations" (pp. 21–22). We believe the same thing can be said about novice teachers; they, too, struggle with forging a professional identity that must meet a variety of expectations and needs.

We aim, then, with our collection to foster the development of ways of thinking like a more expert teacher to assist preservice and novice teachers as they make the transition from instructional consumer to instructional leader. As Darling-Hammond points out, teaching is a complicated, complex endeavor, necessitating adaptive expertise and the ability to fulfill multiple roles simultaneously. We add to this characterization of teaching the realities of the learning environment in which it occurs, realities that often include unanticipated occurrences, from minor to serious, that can derail the plans of even the most prepared and proficient practitioners.

USING NOVICE TEACHER NARRATIVES TO PRACTICE
THINKING LIKE AN EXPERT TEACHER

However, our book raises a key question: Can a new teacher be taught to teach like an expert after only four years of undergraduate or even fewer years of graduate courses and a few school site-based field experiences? In "What Malcolm Gladwell Got Wrong from the Author of the 10,000 Hours Study," David Burkus (2016) shares what he learned from interviewing Anders Ericsson about his study of Berlin violinists made famous as the "10,000-rule" in Malcolm Gladwell's book *Outliers*.

Burkus writes that, according to Ericsson, those who practiced for ten thousand hours showed promise, but

> perhaps most important, [the] distinction between what Gladwell popularized and what Ericsson's research showed is that it's not about hours of practice, it's about *deliberate* practice: "That's a kind of practice where you're not actually doing your job, you're actually taking time where you're focusing in on trying to improve," Ericsson says. "In particular, when you do that under the guidance of a master teacher, so the teacher would be able to actually tell you what is going to be the next step here in your development. That is the kind of practice that we talked about as being essential to reach the highest level of performance." Gladwell and Ericsson agree that talent is the product of *rigorous* practice. (Burkus, para. 6; emphasis added)

So, if we believe what Ericsson concludes about expert musicians, the question for us is can we create a parallel environment for novice teachers that includes deliberate and rigorous practice under the guidance of master teachers that will promote and sustain more promising and gifted teachers? We should, or at the very least, we need to try; introducing early teaching narratives in our teacher education programs may be one way to accomplish this goal.

A FRAMEWORK FOR ORGANIZING THE NARRATIVES

We have organized the chapters in our collection into parts that correspond to Charlotte Danielson's *Framework for Teaching*. The Framework is

> a research-based set of components of instruction, aligned to the Interstate Teacher Assessment Consortium (InTASC) Standards, and grounded in a constructivist view of learning and teaching. The complex activity of teaching is divided into 22 components (and 76 smaller elements) clustered into four domains of teaching responsibility (The Danielson Group, 2013).

The Danielson Group (2013) suggests that the Framework may be used for many purposes, but that "its full value is realized as the foundation for professional conversations among practitioners as they seek to enhance their skill in the complex task of teaching."

For this study, we used the version of Danielson's Framework that our teacher candidates were familiar with, as it is required reading for clinical experiences: Danielson's "Domains, Components, and Elements of the Framework for Teaching" from *Enhancing Professional Practice: A Framework for Teaching* (2007). These four domains are Planning and Preparation, Classroom Environment, Instruction, and Professional Responsibilities, and each domain includes related components and elements (see appendix A).

Our teacher candidates study and apply these domains throughout their years of teacher preparation at our university, and they are required to pass an assessment rated by their university supervisors with a Pennsylvania Department of Education (n.d.) form that uses the Danielson Framework at midterm and at the end of their fifteen-week student teaching experience in order to be certified in our state.

OUR METHODOLOGY

We sent out a call for proposals to recent graduates of our English education program, those who had been teaching for five years or fewer, to write about any experience, issue, or problem they had encountered during student teaching or their first years of teaching that was memorable for them or made a distinct impression upon them. After fifteen graduates sent us their stories and we read them, we asked them to reread what they had written and, using the Danielson Framework, to consider how the four domains were reflected in their narratives (see appendix A).

After our writers completed this second step, we interviewed each one face-to-face or by phone, Skype, or e-mail, asking each one the same questions:

1. Looking at the Danielson domains you selected in your reflection, which of the components described in that domain are reflected by your situation and the choices you made?
2. Are there any domains or components from them that you didn't mention in your reflective response that you would like to add at this time?
3. Could you explain further what you meant by (we chose selected quotations from each narrative) in your writing?

4. Did rereading your narrative and looking at it again with Danielson's domains in mind raise any other questions for you?
5. Looking back again at the experience you shared, what, if anything, would
   you do differently now?
6. Is there anything else you'd like to add about what you have written?

Each chapter, then, includes a teacher narrative, a reflection with reference
to the Danielson lens, Linda's or Jo-Anne's summary of the follow-up interview, a commentary written by Jo-Anne or Linda, and prompts for reflection,
discussion questions, and suggestions for inquiry and additional reading.

OVERVIEW OF THE COLLECTION

Our decision to utilize Danielson's domains as a means for categorizing our
narratives was informed by Danielson's belief that although teaching is a
complex endeavor, there is value in a "common language for professional
conversation" (p. 5) and a means by which to "definitively describe good
practice" (2007, p. 6).

However, we also recognize that this organizational template has limita-
tions. What will become apparent almost immediately to our readers is that
each narrative in the collection mirrors more than one domain, something
that all our contributors note as well in their reflections and interviews. Thus,
although we use the Framework as a convenient way to organize this collection, and we have placed each narrative in one of the four domain headings
we thought was most dominant, we nonetheless understand that teaching is
much more than the sum of its parts—or domains.

Furthermore, similar to our writers in this collection, as mentors and as
teacher educators, we also made choices about what we noticed in each of
these narratives and made decisions about what to suggest or advise in their
situations; our readers may have additional responses to each of our teachers'
experiences and additional resources they would suggest; so allow yourselves
to be placed in these classrooms and consider what choices you would make
using your own situational pedagogy while discussing our reflections and
questions.

Prior to the sections and their corresponding narratives, we include the
preface written by Sara, whose experience, as we explain above, was the catalyst for our study. In this preface, Sara relates the story that she shared with
Jo-Anne that opened up a discussion about the need for teacher preparation
programs to better prepare teacher candidates for the realities of teaching in
today's classrooms.

Following the other fifteen narratives, Sara's afterword includes her thoughts about this experience informed by a re-examination of Danielson's Framework, illustrating a deeper understanding of how effective teachers function, followed by a jointly written commentary by Linda and Jo-Anne. The preface and afterword thus function as bookends to the collection. We conclude this text with thoughts on what this project has taught us as teacher educators and how we can contribute to the ongoing and ever-changing process of teacher development.

The four narratives in Part I, "Planning and Preparation," demonstrate the many considerations new teachers make before they teach. While the components and elements that are subsumed within this domain delineate the various considerations that teachers must take into account as they put their pedagogical content knowledge to use before teaching their lessons, the stories shared in this section highlight the synergistic relationship that this domain has with the other domains in Danielson's Framework.

Ian Cunningham's story of meticulously planning a lesson for his seventh graders, a lesson that would be observed by his building principal, reminds us that responsive teaching means that sometimes well-designed lessons must be abandoned when the usual school day is disrupted by two words: "early dismissal."

Samantha DiMauro shares some insights into the importance of making sure that knowledge of content and pedagogy is augmented by knowledge of students when planning lessons while also reminding teachers of the importance of persevering despite student apathy and apparent disengagement, thus adding another dimension to the notion of professionalism.

Emily DuPlessis's narrative presents a realistic depiction of a day in the life of a teacher who, despite her attention to making sure that she had sufficient time to prepare for a new lesson, found herself scrambling to do so as she struggled to balance planning and preparation with the need to fulfill other demands placed upon her. For Emily, integrity and ethical conduct emerge as significant aspects of her professional identity.

Finally, Alex Hagood's story about a "failure" of technology reminds us that teachers can likewise fail if they don't have an alternative plan ready when a lesson is dependent upon some form of technology. In Alex's case, his lack of forethought had adverse effects not only on his lesson but also on classroom management.

Part II, "The Classroom Environment," presents two narratives that emphasize building classroom communities and the essential task of creating the proper and appropriate space so learning can occur.

Scott Gibbons's and Heather Lowry's stories focus on relationships and interactions between teachers and their students. Scott sees a direct connection between his efforts to establish rapport with his students and their academic achievement. Scott students do well, he believes, because he cares. And behavior management problems are diminished, too, when care is taken to build and maintain caring relationships with students.

Like Scott, Heather believes that effective teachers are caring teachers, and she shares her belief in the ability of caring teachers to help both at-risk learners and learners who place high value on extracurricular activities. Heather also points out that good teachers wear many "hats" while she explains how the domains manifest themselves in every aspect of her teaching.

The four contributions to Part III, "Instruction," reveal insights about what they taught and how they taught, and come to terms with circumstances that are not always within their control.

Shane Conrad's narrative, "A Horse to Water," presents readers with a heartbreakingly real picture of teaching in an impoverished, inadequately supported school beset with problems and challenges that any teacher would find daunting. Looking back at this first year of teaching and its many challenges, Shane realizes that he learned a great deal that he is now using to be the "best damn teacher" he can be and that he will continue to grow as a teacher. Instruction does not occur in a vacuum; it is affected by a variety of issues and situations, some of which cannot be controlled by the teacher.

One of the realities of teaching today is that teachers are not always autonomous (or trusted to develop their own curricula) something that Richard Courtot makes clear as he tells us about an experience he had as a long-term substitute during "A Tumultuous First Year." Tasked with implementing scripted lessons, Ricky thought long and hard about how to proceed and how to retain his agency as a teacher.

In "Teaching to an Empty Desk," Edward Litzinger states an obvious point: "teaching an empty desk is impossible," thus highlighting the challenge of chronic student absenteeism, while acknowledging the complexities of this problem for both students and teachers. For Ed, though, absenteeism (and other challenges present in today's classrooms) can't result in teachers throwing in the towel. In fact, he realizes that there are ways and means for teachers to reach out to chronically absent students that may encourage them to attend school regularly.

"An Unexpected Teachable Moment" by Michael Tosti demonstrates that careful planning must occasionally give way to the needs of students and to the unpredictable directions that authentic discussions can take. Michael reminds us that teachers will always face unexpected moments that demand flexibility, demonstrating the necessity for responsive teaching. For Michael, engaging students in learning means being able to take advantage of unanticipated events that can foster learning.

The five narratives in Part IV, "Professional Responsibilities," address the multiple professional roles new teachers adopt as they engage with students and as they mature within the larger world of school outside their own individual classrooms.

In "Teacher-Parent," Tara Brodish states that although she was prepared to be a teacher to her students, she wasn't prepared to be a "parent" to them. Tara discovered that she was often called upon to fulfill this role because some of her students didn't have parents who were present in their lives. In retrospect, she realizes the importance of establishing a rapport with students, as this rapport has significant effects on instruction and the learning environment. Tara's story also shows facets of professional responsibilities that new teachers may not think about initially—service and advocacy.

Nicole Frankenfield discovered that on some days teachers must teach lessons that help their students make it through a difficult time and reminds readers of the importance of listening to students, a point she clearly demonstrates in "Lessons That 'Stick.'" Thinking about her story later, she realizes that all students have "baggage" that can affect their learning; baggage that can't be left at the classroom door and thus often has an effect on teachers' planning and preparation as well as the environment of the classroom. Like Tara, Nicole presents us with a story that puts professional responsibility front and center.

As a student teacher, Patrick Gahagan was welcomed into a community in which teachers and administrators dedicated themselves to ensuring that all students could be successful. However, as he relates in "Teaching a Student with Depression," when he found himself working with a student who suffered from depression and anxiety, he realized just how challenging this effort can be. Looking back on his experience with Ali, he realized the importance of integrating her into the classroom community while noting the importance of a "network" consisting of Ali's teachers, her mother, the school guidance counselor, and assistant principal that collaborated to meet Ali's needs.

In "The Pang of Terror," Janel Prinkey writes about teaching amid crises that occur without any notice, noting that these challenges are part of being a teacher and that, for her, they resulted in greater confidence in her abilities. In her reflection, Janel asserts that whatever teachers do, they have to do it as a professional while noting the great responsibilities that teaching entails outside of knowing and being able to teach the subject matter.

Middle school English language arts teacher Caroline Lehman's story, "Defending and Protecting My Students," resonates in this era of concerns about school safety and security. Having undergone ALICE (Alert, Lockdown, Inform, Counter, Evacuate) training, she shares the discovery of her role as protector and defender of her charges and the effects of this discovery on her understandings of professional responsibilities and her sense of professional identity. In retrospect, Caroline draws an important and disturbing conclusion—that as she works to create a welcoming and open space in her room, ALICE training is also asking her to think about how she might fortify and weaponize this same environment.

We now invite you to read the preface of our collection in which Sara recounts the story that got us started on this journey to discover how we could help preservice and novice teachers successfully meet the challenges and vagaries of today's classrooms. While Sara's narrative recounts events that would tax even a more experienced teacher, it nonetheless effectively captures the realities of day-to-day teaching. This is where we begin. We encourage you, our readers, however, to use this text in any order that is most helpful and most useful to you in learning new ways of thinking like a teacher.

REFERENCES

Alsup, J. (2006). *Teacher identity discourses: Negotiating personal and professional spaces*. Mahwah, NJ: Lawrence Earlbaum Associates.

Blau, S. (2003). *The literature workshop: Teaching texts and their readers*. Portsmouth, NH: Heinemann.

Brent, D. (2012). Crossing boundaries: Co-op students relearning to write. *College Composition and Communication, 63*, 558–92.

Britzman, D. P. (2003). *Practice makes practice: A critical study of learning to teach*. 2nd ed. Albany: State University of New York Press.

Bruner, J. (1986). *Actual minds, possible worlds*. Cambridge: Harvard University Press.

Burkus, D. (2016). What Malcolm Gladwell got wrong, from the author of the 10,000 hours study. Retrieved from http://www.inc.com/david-burkus/what-malcolm-gladwell-missed-about-the-10000-hour-rule.html.

Conference on English Education. (2016). What do we know and believe about the roles of methods courses and field experiences in English education? Retrieved from http://www.ncte.org/cee/positions/roleofmethodsinee.

Council of Chief State Officers. InTASC model core standards and learning progressions for teachers. (2012). Retrieved from http://www.ccsso.org/Documents/2013/2013_INTASC_Learning_Progressions_for_Teachers.pdf.

Danielson, C. (2007). *Enhancing professional practice: A framework for teaching*. Alexandria, VA: Association for Supervision and Curriculum Development.

Darling-Hammond, L. (2006). *Powerful teacher education: Lessons from exemplary programs*. San Francisco: Jossey-Bass.

Fioriello, P. (2015). 4 real reasons teachers leave the profession. Retrieved from http://drpfconsults.com/4-real-reasons-why-teachers-leave-the-profession/.

Katz, L. G., & Raths, J. D. (1985). Disposition as goals for teacher education. *Teaching and Teacher Education, 1*(4), 301–7.

Kerr, J., & Norris, L. (2008). Community, collegiality, collaboration: Creating and sustaining productive relationships with cooperating teachers. *The Field Experience Journal, 2*, 76–90.

Kerr, J., & Norris, L. (2010). "Wondering" through teaching: How building reflective practice and the teacher work sample help pre-service teachers develop inquiring minds. *The Field Experience Journal, 3*, 36–64.

Mahiri, J., & Freedman, S. W. (2014). *The first year of teaching: Classroom research to increase student learning.* New York: Teachers College Press.

McCarthy, J., & Norris, L. (2013). Keeping candidates safe: School safety and prevention of violence for preservice teachers. Position paper. Pennsylvania Association of Colleges and Teacher Educators. Retrieved from https://www.pac-te.org/i4a/doclibrary/index.cfm?category_id=5.

McCutcheon, G. (1992). Facilitating teacher personal theorizing. In E. W. Ross, J. W. Cornett, and G. McCutcheon (Eds.), *Teacher personal theorizing* (pp. 191–206). Albany: State University of New York Press.

Miller, sj, & Norris, L. (2007). *Unpacking the loaded teacher matrix: Negotiating space and time between university and secondary English classrooms.* New York: Peter Lang.

Pennsylvania Department of Education. (n.d.). 430 form. Retrieved from http://www.education.pa.gov/Documents/Teachers-Administrators/Certifications/Fees%20and%20Forms/PDE%20430.pdf.

Schon, D. A. (1995). Causality and causal inference in the study of organizations. In Goodman, R. E. & W. R. Fisher (Eds.), *Rethinking knowledge: Reflections across the disciplines* (pp. 69–102). Albany: State University of New York Press.

Schussler, D. L. (2006). Defining dispositions: Wading through murky waters. *The Teacher Educator, 41*, 251–68.

Smagorinsky, P. (2008). *Teaching English by design: How to create and carry out instructional units.* Portsmouth, NH: Heinemann.

Tishman, S., E. Jay, & D. N. Perkins. (1993). Teaching thinking dispositions: From transmission to enculturation. Retrieved from http://citeseerx.ist.psu.edu/viewdoc/download;jsessionid=1CDBD770FAA1879FFE8A3418FC57E4A4?doi=10.1.1.23.7880&rep=rep1&type=pdf.

The Danielson Group II. (2013). The framework. Retrieved from https://www.danielsongroup.org/framework/.

Trimmer, J. (1997). *Narration as knowledge: Tales of the teaching life.* Portsmouth, NH: Heinemann.

Yancey, K. B. (2004). *Teaching literature as reflective practice.* Urbana, IL: NCTE.

Part I

PLANNING AND PREPARATION

Planning and Preparation comprises the teacher candidates' or new teachers' knowledge of both content and pedagogy, knowledge that must be accompanied by understanding of students and familiarity with available resources. Planning coherent instruction with clear instructional outcomes suitable for diverse learners and with formative and summative assessments in place is also included.

Chapter One

Of Early Dismissals and Observations

Ian Cunningham

With insight and humor, Ian describes teaching middle schoolers on a day when there is an unexpected early dismissal as he was preparing to be observed by the building principal.

As a 2012 English education graduate, I had been schooled about the Danielson Framework for Teaching throughout my college education courses and particularly in my methods courses. So when it came time for my first-ever formal observation from my building principal, I put all of my Danielson know-how to good use in my lesson design.

"I'll impress this guy!" I thought.

I was in the middle of teaching my seventh graders a unit on theme, and we had just finished reading Piri Thomas's short story, "Amigo Brothers." The students had really enjoyed the story, so I created a game called "Theme Lawyers" in which groups of four would reread the story and defend predetermined themes with textual evidence. They would later present their evidence to a "jury of peers" (their classmates).

After spending countless hours obsessing over the details of this lesson, I felt extremely prepared for my observation. I even changed the "Name" line of the students' document to "The Law Offices of . . ."

"A perfectly cute touch!" I thought.

Bring in the principal!

And I did bring in the principal. He came during my fifth period, which had just been reduced from 53 minutes to 32. The reason for this? An ice storm was working its way nearer by the second, and the district would be dismissing students two hours early.

The dismissal announcement had been made at the *end of fourth period*, and students would be dismissed for the day at the *end of fifth period*. There was a deafening cacophony of celebratory cries accompanied by dancing. Students screamed in the hallways and rolled on the floors.

I was sick to my stomach.

My principal, an amiable, straightforward guy, gave me a less-than-encouraging heads-up on the way in the door: "Sorry about the circumstances. I considered rescheduling this observation altogether, but I know I already did that once to you. If this dismissal situation creates a problem for this class, we'll try it again after Thanksgiving."

The early dismissal did create a problem. My fifth period had twenty-seven students in it, and many were rowdy or off-task on their best days. I didn't have enough time to get through all elements of the lesson; students were uninterested and lackadaisical, and I could not keep them on-task.

The teamwork period of instruction was spent with students making after-school plans and discussing the excitement of the dismissal. Some didn't even open their books.

When the bell rang, my principal looked at me with frustration.

"Sorry I even came in today, Ian" he said. "Let's just try this again in a week or two. I'll send you an e-mail."

Needless to say, I took no joy in the early dismissal. I left work feeling defeated and sick, as icy and gray as the weather outside.

I'd like to say that I went home and forgot about the debacle at work, or that I shook it off as being what it was: a situation coupled with some bad luck and bad timing. I sulked in my frustration for a while. This was my career on the line, and I felt as though I had failed. It wasn't my first classroom failure, but this time it really seemed to matter. My supervisor had witnessed it.

I had another observation, this time under much more normal circumstances. I was observed teaching a lesson on "Multiple-Meaning Words" in a poetry unit while using a ReadWriteThink video produced by Radiolab. Students were engaged and participatory, and everything went just fine. When I got my observation results, everything was kosher.

After my satisfactory observation, I didn't drive home mentally celebrating my successes. Nor did I reflect on the great work of my students that day. I didn't call my family and express my joy and relief. I was just glad the pressure had lessened. Glad that's over. *"Now what should I worry about next?"*

Vagaries, new ones popping up all the time, make teaching the challenging career that it is. We cannot control the unexpected shifts in the classroom environment; however, we can control our responses to them. In controlling our responses, we can take a clearer look at our actual effectiveness and improve as we gain experience.

As a teacher, you will find that adaptability is a "make-or-break" asset. Adapting relates to more than just lesson planning and managing student behavior, as unexpected events come in many forms. In the long run, it is more important to be clearheaded and able to critically evaluate and adapt after instruction than it is to execute without deviation the best-laid plans all the time.

Take a moment to think about something important that you learned from reading Ian's story Why is this learning important to you as a preservice teacher?

IAN'S REFLECTION

Thinking about my story again with Danielson's Framework in mind, I realize that knowledge of some aspects of the Danielson model could have aided my decision-making on the day of my observation. Although the framework is a great way to conceptualize practice, it does not take into account the unexpected problems that can come about.

I should have asked my principal to reschedule my observation after finding out that the period would be cut short. With the observation not a factor to consider, I would have then adapted for the shortened period with a different activity altogether or a shortened or introductory version of my original plan.

My primary areas of professional growth fall under Danielson's subdomains 1b: (Demonstrating Knowledge of Students) and 4d (Participating in a Professional Community). In the 1b area, I now know the behaviors of my seventh graders well enough to determine that some are not going to perform at a proficient observable level if they are being unexpectedly dismissed for the day in twenty minutes.

I can attest that I have grown secure in my own establishment as a professional (Component 4d: Participating in a Professional Community). This is to say that I would not feel uncomfortable now simply explaining to the principal that I did not want to be observed during that period, or why I felt it was not fair to be observed that period.

At the time of the experience, I overplayed the significance of the observation to the point where my thinking (before and after the ice storm debacle) was detrimental. While my lesson had merits, I was indeed trying to overplay some simple details in an effort to impress rather than give a snapshot of a normal class day (if there is such a thing). This effort, coupled with the weather event and general turbulence of the day, may have confused some of my students.

Revisiting the experience has helped me realize that I should have thought more carefully about adapting my teaching that day rather than trying to impress my principal.

IAN'S INTERVIEW WITH JO-ANNE

Ian shared additional ideas about and insights into his narrative during our interview. Reiterating what he wrote in his reflection, Ian stated what was now quite obvious—that he should have asked his principal to reschedule the observation. But he stated, "He was my evaluator and I was afraid."

He also talked about how his experience with this observation and evaluation relates to Domain 4: Professional Responsibilities, especially Component 4f: Showing Professionalism, one element of which is "compliance with school and district regulations." Ian believes that being a professional means being aware of observation and evaluation requirements; however, he is also aware of the weaknesses of the system in place at his school and district regarding observations of teaching.

For Ian, at best, it (an observation) only provides a "snapshot" of one's teaching. However, at the same time he referred to Component 4e: Growing and Developing Professionally, in particular to "receptivity to feedback from colleagues." While Ian understands the limits of evaluative observations of teachers, he nonetheless perceives their value as well.

Additionally, Ian expressed a renewed understanding of Domain 3, Component 3e: Demonstrating Flexibility and Responsiveness, in particular, "lesson adjustments." Ian believes that at the time he didn't have sufficient experience to be as flexible as the situation demanded. Now, though, he has an "arsenal" from which he can draw when the need arises.

Ian made an additional important point, stating that although novice teachers may believe that careful attention to Domain 1: Planning and Preparation will ensure effective teaching and student learning, the reality is that "good lessons" don't always work and that planning and preparation are always susceptible to the vagaries of the school day.

Finally, Ian observed that while efficient use of instructional time is key, controlling that instructional time is often out of teachers' hands. Certainly, having a class period cut short by twenty minutes, with no advance warning, demonstrates this lack of control quite dramatically.

JO-ANNE'S COMMENTARY

Ian's narrative captures one constant of teaching—that it is susceptible to, and can even be undermined by, unexpected events. For Ian, a change in the bell schedule as a result of an early dismissal went beyond a mere annoyance because of a scheduled observation, resulting in stress, second guessing, and unwarranted worry.

The formation of a professional identity is especially critical during the first years of teaching. This construction is tricky, as it is, among other things, contingent upon social negotiation (Danielwicz, 2001, p. 10). As Ian eventually realized, he should have asked his principal to reschedule the observation; however, this option did not occur to him at the time because he was working to establish a relationship with the principal.

As a novice teacher, Ian's understanding of this relationship meant that he had to comply and that he had no other options available. Remember that Ian perceived his principal as an "evaluator" and that he wanted to make a good impression, despite the fact that the time during which he was going to make this good impression had been reduced by twenty minutes.

Ian's ways of thinking about this relationship changed, though, and now he realizes that he can be "upfront" about his needs. Constructing a professional identity, then, also entails an evolution in ways of thinking—in this case thinking related to the relationship between administrator and teacher. Thus, we see Domain 4, Component 4d: Participating in a Professional Community reflected, one element of which includes "relationships with colleagues." Ian's principal is not a colleague; however, there exists a collegial relationship between principals and teachers, given their shared goals and concerns.

Ian's narrative, reflection, and concluding thoughts demonstrate that novice teachers' professional identities are in flux, a result, in part, of institutional demands and the work involved with building relationships with students, colleagues, and administration. And, of course, there is also the continuous work to develop expertise and to augment pedagogical content knowledge going on simultaneously.

Ian's thinking also demonstrates a deeper understanding of responsive teaching, being responsive to learners' needs but also being responsive to the context in which teaching occurs. Being responsive and flexible when the situation demands means being better able to meet learners' needs. Ian noted that now, as a more experienced teacher, he has an "arsenal" of teaching ideas that he can pull from when the need arises, but, also, he's thinking differently about the decision to abandon original plans. In short, Ian is thinking like an expert teacher—realizing the futility of going forward with plans when the situation demands otherwise.

Furthermore, in Ian's reflection and interview we find evidence of a more nuanced understanding of effective practice. Plugging this lesson into a much abbreviated class period did not work. Ian now knows that best practice does not exist in a vacuum, impervious to novel situations and unreasonable time constraints. Best practices need to be accompanied by teachers' own theorizing. As Danielwicz (2001) asserts, "Teaching entails invention and adaptation; nothing can be transferred directly from one social context to another" (p. 159).

Finally, some information about the teacher evaluation system in place in Pennsylvania, where Ian teaches, may explain Ian's anxiety over the observation and his desire to make a good impression.

Teachers with fewer than three years of satisfactory teaching are evaluated twice each school year. The evaluation is evidence-based and aligned with the domains that Danielson sets forth in the Framework. Subsequent to observations, teachers meet with their observer to be scored in each of the subdomains. All of the scoring is done in an interactive online system, the Electronic Teacher Evaluation Portal.

Teachers provide evidence to justify scores by uploading documents and responding to pre- and post-observation questions that are aligned with the domains. Teachers also self-assess each of the subdomain areas using a score of 0–3, with 0 meaning failing, 1 meaning needs improvement, 2 meaning proficient, and 3 meaning advanced. Teachers and principals then discuss any inconsistencies in scores that they arrived at during their post-observation meeting. Ultimately, principals decide on scores; however, there is room for negotiation or challenge to a score or scores.

Non-tenured teachers who receive more than one unsatisfactory observation (a holistic, combined observation rating of under 2, the proficient mark), can be terminated. Most likely, if it is determined that a teacher is not proficient after one observation, then that teacher will be put on a "plan of improvement" through the Pennsylvania Department of Education Standards Aligned System where they are required to complete a battery of reflection assignments outlining how they plan to improve. This plan also entails meetings with administrators and observations of other classrooms, among other things. Thus, there was a lot at stake for Ian.

FOR DISCUSSION

1. Did your understandings of any of Danielson's domains change or deepen as a result of reading Ian's narrative and reflection? Explain. If your understandings of the domains did not change or deepen, which domain, component, and/or element emerged as especially significant to you?

2. Ian shares that he now has an "arsenal" of lesson ideas that he can use when the need arises. What are some lessons that you might have in your "arsenal" that you can use when you are unable to teach a lesson that you were planning? For instance, perhaps, like Ian, there is a change in the bell schedule which means that you will be meeting with your students for 20 minutes rather than 50. Or there is a field trip and half of your students are missing. It's "school picture day" and students are being called out of class to have their photos taken.

FOR REFLECTION

As a student, you developed an understanding of the role of the building principal based upon your status as "instructional consumer." How have your understandings of the role of the building principal evolved as you transition to "educational leader"? As you reflect, consider these questions: What have you learned about the responsibilities that principals are tasked with? What support can you reasonably expect from a building principal? What might you do to ensure a good working relationship with your building principal?

FOR INQUIRY

Investigate the procedures for teacher evaluation in a state in which you would like to teach. Provide an overview of the evaluation system and a critique of its validity. Upon what understanding of effective teaching is the system based? If standards are referenced, which standards are they?

SUGGESTED READING

Goldstein, D. (2015). *The teacher wars: A history of America's most embattled profession*. New York: Anchor Books.

Marzano, R. J., & Toth, M. D. (2013). *Teacher evaluation that makes a difference: A new model for teacher growth and student achievement*. Alexandria, VA: Association for Supervision and Curriculum Development.

Chapter Two

One Size Never Fits All

Teaching the Same
Lesson with Differing Outcomes

Samantha DiMauro

Samantha's narrative focuses on lesson planning for two different secondary grade levels as well as how to motivate students who may be uninterested in and disconnected from the topic.

I was given the opportunity to construct and teach a two-day lesson on interpersonal communication for two public speaking classes, seventh and twelfth grade. Due to my lack of knowledge on the subject, this was a rather difficult yet fun experience for me. Since my cooperating teacher knew a lot about communication and media, I asked her for some guidance on how to find examples and the best way to define interpersonal communication to a group of students who did not know the meaning.

I was also able to conduct some research of my own and found not only the different styles of communication but some video clips that went along with my lessons to help students understand the meaning and provide some examples that would help them later on with their individual speeches. It was interesting how different the lessons became when I began teaching them.

I had more trouble with the twelfth grade students because of their lack of motivation. Since it was their senior year, they were having a difficult time accepting the fact that they had to participate in class and complete all assignments. Most of the struggle was not from their inability to understand the material but their feelings about how ridiculous it was for them to complete the assignment that was given to them.

Due to their lack of interest in participating in class, I decided that the best thing to do would be to give them an activity to do while watching a video clip the next day. I wanted students to know that they are accountable for their successes in the classroom, and the only way to do that, at the time, was to give them an activity that was relevant not only to the lesson but to the overall focus of the public speaking class.

I was pleasantly surprised with the seventh grade class because of their enthusiasm and willingness to learn and participate. They were ready to contribute and give examples when needed, which made it easier to have a class discussion. Their enthusiasm made it easier to present a lesson on a subject they weren't too knowledgeable about and to use answers they gave me to keep the lesson going.

Much like the senior public speaking class, I had to come up with an activity on the second day which would demonstrate to the seventh graders the importance of being accountable for their learning. This was a great way for me to see how well I was communicating information that was new to students and indicate where and what I needed to work on as a teacher.

This was a revealing experience because it allowed me to identify the differences in both age groups. Prior to student teaching, I was adamant about teaching seniors because I felt that I would be able to do more with them in the classroom (i.e., discussions, presentations, etc.), however, I soon realized that students in that particular age group are more concerned with finishing high school as quickly as possible, and in some cases, with as minimal work as possible.

I was pleasantly surprised with the seventh graders because they seemed to enjoy the assignment and wanted to participate more in discussion. I learned that although the presentation of information may be the same, each group is going to respond in their own way based on their willingness to learn and to complete the assignments.

My narrative should help pre-service teachers who are struggling to understand why their lesson didn't work or feeling as if they aren't able to connect with their students. Regardless of the age group, students will make it known that they aren't interested in a topic or don't want to complete the assignments. It is our responsibility as educators to continue educating students and providing them with the tools needed to succeed; and even if they don't understand the benefits of the assignment or lesson at the time it is taught, they may someday use and value what is given to them either in the workplace or in college.

Before reading Samantha's reflection, consider the following questions:

1. Were you surprised that the seventh and twelfth graders responded differently or with how each grade level reacted to Samantha's communication lesson? Why or why not?

2. Can or should lesson plans be the same for junior high and senior high students when the content knowledge, as in this case on styles of communication and interpersonal communication, is the same? Explain.

SAMANTHA'S REFLECTION

As I read my reflection with Danielson's Framework in mind, it was clear that my attention was on finding something to keep the seniors busy. This could have been avoided by taking into consideration the students' interests and prior knowledge of interpersonal communication, using each to create a lesson that would increase student involvement. It was difficult to keep seniors engaged, which resulted in creating an assignment to keep them from complaining about the work.

There are a few ways I could have approached this class differently. I had general knowledge about the students, but I did not know too much about their interests, except for the sports they played and some extracurricular activities. Additional knowledge about their skills as learners could have helped in creating a lesson that gained their interest. More research should have been conducted on how to present the new material to students and how to create mini-discussions that were more student centered.

As I considered helping students create a space that allows them to freely discuss the content, I realized the introduction of a video clip could help in assessing student understanding of new material. The video clip would allow students to use their knowledge and apply it to real-life situations, which could lead to further discussion on the role that interpersonal communication serves in our lives.

If students are given the opportunity to take an active role in their learning, then they will be more receptive when presented with new concepts. Although this may not always occur, it gives them a sense of responsibility and it helps to create an environment that facilitates discussion.

SAMANTHA'S INTERVIEW WITH LINDA

Samantha shared that it was quite an experience to teach both the youngest and the oldest students at her school site. She began by referring to Domain 1: Planning and Preparation, specifically, Component 1b, Demonstrating Knowledge of Students, Knowledge of Child and Adolescent Development, explaining that she was "taught how to teach" but felt she was missing the understanding of adolescents in how a seventh grader was different from a twelfth grader. If she would have known more about the seniors, who were almost eighteen, she wouldn't have created "busy work" for them; she stated, "Worksheets to keep them quiet didn't work."

She also related to bulleted item 4, Knowledge of Students' Interest and Cultural Heritage, learning some students' extracurricular interests and activities but not much more about them and explaining that the second week of the semester is not a lot of time to get to know students. She compared that her direct instruction to the seventh graders during her second period class worked well, but for the fourth period senior class, she should have turned the lesson into a group discussion "like for freshmen in college." She went on to say that she should have "turned it over to them taking over their own learning," while "I'm overseeing."

Other domains of importance to Samantha were 2b: Establishing a Culture for Learning; 3b: Using Questioning and Discussion Techniques; and 3c: Engaging Students in Learning. Samantha thought these three components "would go well together." She said, "I missed the WHY—WHY it [the content] was important."

Looking deeper into the domains, Samantha learned that the expectations have to change for each class (2b. bullet 2, Expectations for Learning and Achievement), and that in her planning she should have considered a different assignment for the seniors such as a group discussion, group project, or group speech (2b. bullet 3, Student Pride in Work).

She also added component 2d: Managing Student Behavior. She explained, "Seniors want to be your friend," and remarked that being only seven years older than they were, she "loved joking with them." But then she added, "The next minute you're serious and you have to say, 'OK, guys, you have to do this.'" She revealed how she has learned to separate herself as teacher and facilitator from her students; she told me that she has to "be friendly, but not your friend."

Samantha touched on Domain 4: Professional Responsibilities, Component 4e: Growing and Developing Professionally, recognizing wisely that as a student teacher, "I still didn't feel like I was the *actual* teacher. The final say comes from the cooperating teacher."

She explained that sometimes a cooperating teacher wants teaching to be done "this way," and she felt that she couldn't "evolve as much as you would like to," being a guest in the school and not really having a classroom of her own yet. She stated emphatically that there is "a lot to digest" in fifteen weeks.

Samantha ended by sharing her understanding of Component 4d: Participating in a Professional Community, point 1, Relationship with Colleagues, that she became close with other teachers in her building and her relationship with colleagues, including her cooperating teacher, was "all useful" and "all helpful" in her journey to becoming a professional.

LINDA'S COMMENTARY

Samantha's narrative examines important considerations new teachers must make when planning and preparing lessons or units, sometimes lessons that will be taught across grade levels. Samantha realized by the second week of her student teaching that she needed to better comprehend how to actively engage her senior class so they would stay motivated and that a one-size-fits-all approach to teaching two different classes wasn't effective. Had she considered the following questions in planning her public speaking lessons, she may have met with better success earlier on.

First and foremost, teachers should ask, "Who are my students?" Subquestions might include:

- How do I engage my students immediately and make my class more student-centered early on?
- How can I motivate students to learn and sustain their motivation?
- What are my students' interests and how can I apply those to my lesson planning?

Second is, "What exactly am I teaching?" And subquestions might be:

- How well do I know this subject?
- Where can I go to learn more about this subject in multiple ways but with a short amount of preparation time?
- What do my students already know about it, and how can I build on what they already know?
- What are the goals or outcomes for this lesson or unit?

And third is, "How do I know that students learned what was taught?" A subquestion for beginning teachers might be:

- What measures do I have in place that will demonstrate student accountability, progress, and success?

Answering these questions during planning might have helped Samantha to avoid the roadblocks she faced when teaching unfamiliar material to two different grade levels. She might have begun both classes by asking her students verbally or asking them to write for two minutes and then share with a partner, What do you already know about interpersonal communication? or What do you think interpersonal communication means?

Later, she may have queried, "What do you already know about the different styles of communication people use?" Expert teachers know that the social construction of knowledge is one significant teaching strategy we can use to engage all our students; raising opening questions like these provides us with a baseline to discuss the content, no matter what grade for secondary students. Samantha, thinking like an expert, posed some alternative ways to get her seniors more excited about learning such as through group discussion, a group project, or group speech rather than just completing worksheets.

Had Samantha tried the technique of finding out what her students already knew and built on that foundation, she may have avoided the apathetic response she first received from her seniors. The seventh graders may have exhibited more enthusiasm because the subject could have been newer for them and may have presented more of a challenge than for the senior class who may have been much more familiar with the terms and definitions.

Samantha recognized quickly that what worked in her approach for one grade was not successful for another. Experts know that successful lesson design varies not only among grade levels but also from class to class and will need spontaneous adjustments as we are in the act of teaching.

Being confident in knowing her content and adding to what her students already knew could have helped Samantha to sell the communication tools lesson better to both groups; often new teachers are asked to teach content that they have not taught before and may not be familiar with. This happens frequently with literature selections they may not have read in their college courses or with subjects like public speaking and communication that are tangential to the English language arts but for which they may not have had major coursework.

Samantha used expert teacher moves in both discussing what her cooperating teacher had taught previously in these lessons and by doing her own research on the subject before she met with her students. One text I have used that I would recommend for Samantha's facilitating class discussions is McCann, Johannessen, Kahn, and Flanagan's *Talking in Class: Using Discussion to Enhance Teaching and Learning* (2006).

In his foreword to McCann's text, George Hillocks Jr. states that this book "is a first in going beyond the superficial conditions of question asking and teacher behavior to examine the conditions of pedagogy and curriculum that are most conducive to the development and maintenance of discussion and inquiry resulting in deep learning over long periods of time" (p. xi). I often mention materials along with the cooperating teacher's suggestions when a student teacher is teaching something for the first time and may need additional resources to assist in her planning.

Samantha acted like an expert when she did not take her seniors complaints about doing the work and their minimalist attitudes during their final year of high school lightly; she kept her expectations high and called for accountability through more student engagement in the activities she designed rather than requiring less or giving up. Her role was to be friendly but to act as the instructor and facilitator for their learning, not a peer.

When Samantha perceived her senior class's disconnections from the subject as lack of interest and motivation, she reacted by upping their accountability through "an activity while watching a video clip." She found this strategy successful and applied it to the seventh grade class as well the next day; she could use some material successfully in both classes, but not all. Samantha realized, as experts know, that when students take an active role in the classroom and when the assignments tap into their interests, they are more motivated to do what is asked of them.

As another possible motivator for students to engage in public speaking, Samantha might have given one or both classes a brief survey to find out some topics they might have wanted to speak about, including some of her own suggested examples, and allowed them a few minutes to share in small groups ideas for some topics even before she began the more instructive part of the lesson.

Rightfully, a student teacher's development, in this case in finding resources for planning lessons and becoming familiar with developmental differences in grade levels, cannot and should not always be as far along as her mentors'; Samantha's narrative reminds us that novice teachers can and should do their research on topics that are unfamiliar to them, adapt lessons and assessments to match adolescent development, and take suggestions and ideas from their more experienced cooperating teachers and colleagues as they are evolving through their practicum.

FOR DISCUSSION

1. Samantha thought she wanted to teach the seniors because she felt she could "do more with them"; she was surprised that this was not the case when she taught the seventh grade class. Do you have preconceived notions about what grade level or the kinds of students you would like to teach? How do we form these suppositions about our future classes? How

can we become more realistic in our expectations of students and what they should be able to do?

2. Take a lesson plan you currently use or have used that is for junior or senior high students and adapt it for the opposite school situation. What adaptations did you have to make and why?

FOR REFLECTION

Jo-Anne and I believe it is important for pre-service teachers to try to have experiences both at the junior high (grades 7–9) and senior high (grades 10–12) levels, if possible, before they begin their employment. Do you agree? What advantages might a new teacher have in the job search and in the first years of teaching if she or he has prior experience at both these levels?

FOR INQUIRY

1. Keep a diary of a few of your own junior and senior high experiences, paying close attention to the physical spaces you occupied (you might want to draw these), what your interests were in and outside of school, and some of the assignments you were given and what you thought about them, as well as the characteristics of yourself as a learner in these two environments.

2. Make a list of school culture films you have seen or watch a few of them again, for example, the Harry Potter series as Harry goes from first to last year at Hogwarts. What did you learn from them in terms of how the media portray school culture at different grade levels? How are they different from the realities of schools you have witnessed?

SUGGESTED READING

McCann, T. M., Johannessen, L. R., Kahn, E., & Flanagan, J. M. (2006). *Talking in class: Using discussion to enhance teaching and learning.* Urbana, IL: NCTE.

Myab, N. (2017). How are you communicating to your team? (n.d.). Retrieved from http://www.brighthubpm.com/methods-strategies/79297-comparing-various-forms-of-communication/.

Skills You Need. (2017). Intercommunication skills. Retrieved from http://www.skillsyouneed.com/ips/interpersonal-communication.html.

Chapter Three

The Best-Laid Plans?

Emily DuPlessis

In her narrative, Emily demonstrates how teachers' "best-laid plans" can be co-opted by the demands of administrators and parents as well as by the time constraints of the school day.

The alarm went off an hour earlier than most work days. I had set my alarm early because I was planning on getting to work early to avoid many of the interruptions that typically come up each day for teachers. I was trying a new activity the following day in my class and I wanted to *ensure* that I had adequate time for preparation for an effective delivery. After my regular morning routine and quick drive to work, I arrived nearly an hour early, excited to have some "quiet" time before my day began.

When I arrived, the parking lot was fairly empty except for the vehicles of the few regular early morning risers. Strolling into the office to check my mailbox, I ran into my principal. After some small talk, he insisted that he speak to me immediately about a student. While I wanted to say no, I walked into his office watching the extra time I had allotted quickly tick away.

Thirty minutes later I walked out of his office. As a teacher who understood early on that I would be constantly pulled in different directions for a variety of unexpected events each day, I reassured myself that I still had a little bit of time to finalize the details. When my planning period came, I was ready to maximize my 42 minutes to guarantee I was ready for my new activity the following day. Since I had spent half of my "early time" with the principal that morning, I hadn't yet checked my e-mail. But I knew I needed to quickly do this. Interim reports had gone home the previous day, and there were three parent e-mails in my inbox waiting for a response. I thought to myself, *I shouldn't open them. I can deal with them later.*

Then I realized that I had to teach the rest of the day and that I had an evening packed full of activities. This was the only time that I could respond until tomorrow. So, I set aside the activity, yet again, to answer the e-mails that I knew would haunt me the rest of the day if I didn't take care of them now, all the while knowing that my prep time was ticking away.

Twenty-two minutes later I glanced at the clock and realized that most of my planning period was gone. When you are dealing with parents' e-mails, especially ones related to their children's grades, it is often not a quick note back. I had to go into my grade book and check what grades the students currently had, what assignments they were missing, and spell all of this out for the concerned parents who deserved my time and expected me to get back to them promptly. When I glanced at the clock again, I only had 20 minutes left to refill my water bottle, go to the bathroom, and make sure all of my stuff was ready for the next period that I taught in a different classroom.

And the new activity that I woke up early to finalize had barely been touched.

I quickly took care of the few things I needed to do and made it back to my room with about 15 minutes left of my planning period. For the entire 15 minutes, I focused on creating groups, putting together the folders for the activity, and making sure the copies were ready to go. With about two minutes left of the period, I gathered my materials for my next class and walked out of my room.

At this point in the day, I had three periods left followed by an evening at my husband's company event. The reality quickly sunk in that I would have to arrive to work early again tomorrow to complete some of the finer details that I had intended on completing *today*. I couldn't help but be frustrated with the outcome of the day, especially when I had planned extra time in advance to prepare. When the school day ended, I made a quick to-do list of everything that was left to finish in the morning so that I wouldn't waste any time when I arrived early the next day.

Luckily, the next morning, I arrived at work early and had no interruptions. I spent the extra time making final edits to the activity and making sure the folders for each group were organized and all of the copies were ready to go.

The new activity went extremely well and the students were engaged and excited about this new way to view a text and the collaborative nature of the activity. As I walked around the room and observed their interactions and discussions, I was reminded why it is important to take the time to create innovative learning opportunities for students. While it is easy for teachers to stick to things that are comfortable or are already created, watching my students engage throughout the day was proof that the extra time, the early mornings, and the frustrations were worth it.

While driving home after work I had some time to reflect on those two days and the planning, preparation and implementation of this new learning opportunity for my students. A couple things came to light. First, I was thankful that I had planned ahead and had not tried to complete everything in one day. Had I waited until the day of the activity to come to work early and get it finalized, I may have had the same interruptions and wouldn't have been ready to effectively execute the lesson for my students. As a result, I might have had to scrap the whole idea or put it off another day or two, which would have left me scrounging for a lesson for that particular day.

Second, the nature of our job requires us to be flexible and to be able to adapt on the fly, not only in the classroom when dealing with students and their antics but also when dealing with the other demands placed upon us. I don't wish to scare you, novice teacher, but rather to inform you about the demands that we face as teachers on a daily basis. Often it will feel that your day has gone awry, but your reaction and adaptability to the unforeseen interruptions that are guaranteed to surface will shape your teaching identity in important ways.

While Emily's story demonstrates the importance of Domain 1: Planning and Preparation, what other domains come to mind as you consider the experience that she relates?

EMILY'S REFLECTION

Most of my narrative lives in Danielson's Domains of Planning and Preparation and Professional Responsibilities. While the experience itself dealt mostly with planning and preparation, the arm of teaching that involves communicating with families and showing professionalism (Domain 4) made the planning and preparation difficult.

The reality is that each domain, along with its components and elements, carries a significant level of importance in the life of an educator. It may have been easy to say no to my principal or leave the e-mails for another day, but the integrity and ethical conduct of a teacher require us to have to balance these four domains on *a daily basis.*

Looking back on this experience, I am not sure what I would have done differently. I still would have respected my principal's request and would have met with him when he asked. Perhaps instead of taking half of my planning period to respond to e-mails, I would have sent a quick e-mail to the parents and explained that I had a busy planning period today and that I would gather all of the information for them and send it the following day. This would have allowed me to utilize most of my planning period for preparing the new activity. At the same time, I still would have been acknowledging the parents' concerns, quickly letting them know that I wanted to make sure I was sending them as much information as would be beneficial.

When I began teaching, and faced the reality of time constraints, it was difficult. I felt as though I had numerous ideas and innovative activities I wanted to implement in my classes to give students the best learning experience I could. Quickly, I realized that there are only twenty-four hours in a day and a life outside of my job and that I would have to prioritize what I do with work as to not let it take over my whole life. As difficult as this has been, this realization has helped me narrow my focus and pay attention to what my students need. Yes, I still create innovative activities that appeal to various learning styles; I just realize that innovation can't happen all at once and that we must always allow adequate time for planning and preparation.

EMILY'S INTERVIEW WITH JO-ANNE

Emily began by noting her decision to defer to her principal's needs over her own needs, thus highlighting a component of Danielson's fourth Domain—4d: Participating in a Professional Community, one element of which is "relationship with colleagues." While Emily's principal was, strictly speaking, not a colleague, there is certainly a collegial relationship that exists between administrators and teachers, given their common goals. Emily went on to point to a need for rapport with administration, seeing this as an aspect of professionalism as well.

Emily also noted the importance of rapport with students, maintaining that it allows teachers to better understand their needs as learners. Although rapport is a component of Domain 2: The Classroom Environment, for Emily, rapport also comes into play in Domain 1: Planning and Preparation and Domain 3: Instruction. Rapport with students informs planning and ensures more effective instruction, enhancing communication with students, and fostering the ability to engage students in learning.

Having a few years of teaching under her belt at this point, Emily is also aware of the many responsibilities and tasks expected of teachers, responsibilities and tasks that often result in teachers throwing up their hands and uttering, "Just let me teach." This teaching reality (myriad responsibilities that go beyond merely teaching) is an important reality for novice teachers to grasp, for, as Emily aptly points out, "wanting to do cool things with students can bump up against the realities of day-to-day teaching and also your own life." She sees a need to "strike a balance."

Finally, Emily saw in her own story evidence for the need to consider how actions might be affected by unanticipated situations. Although she was clearly aware of the necessity of devoting extra time to preparing for a new activity, making room in her school day for this extra time did not, in this case, provide the additional time she needed.

JO-ANNE'S COMMENTARY

The portion of Emily's story that focuses on her on-the-spot decision to agree to discuss with her principal a student, despite her need to get started preparing for her new lesson, brings to light a key facet of teaching, that of one's identity as a teacher. Danielwicz (2001) claims that, "becoming a teacher means that an individual must adopt an identity as such" (p. 9). Identity is an understanding of who we are and also who we think others are; thus, we have reflected in Emily's narrative her understanding of herself as teacher at the point in time she describes and her understanding of her principal's identity.

Also, the concept of identity subsumes a few important characteristics: identities are always changing, always varied, and always being constructed (Danielwicz, 2 col, p. 10). Finally, and particularly germane for our discussion here, is that the "taking up of an identity is a constant and tricky social negotiation" (Britzman, 2003, p. 54).

Having established that being a teacher means forming and constructing an identity as such, it is likewise important to note that the "tricky social negotiation" that must occur is just that—tricky. As Miller and Norris (2007) point out, the identities of preservice teachers (and we would add that of novice teachers) are "vulnerable to being co-constructed by competing agendas" while they are also "predetermined because of institutional and social expectations" (pp. 21–22).

A novice teacher, Emily had clear understandings of one facet of her identity—not only being well prepared for lessons but also being a creative, innovative practitioner. Yet, at the same time, this understanding of her identity as a professional came into conflict with another aspect of her identity—professionalism. In an instant, Emily made a choice and acquiesced to institutional expectations—deferring to her principal's needs, suggesting her belief in the importance of a good rapport with administration.

A little later, she made another choice, to respond to parents' e-mails (Domain 4c: Communicating with Families), seeing this as a professional responsibility that had to take precedence over preparation and planning. The "competing agendas" to which Miller and Norris allude are certainly demonstrated by Emily's story as well as Danielwicz's (2001) characterization of teaching as "a complex and delicate act" (p. 9). Danielson's Framework for teaching, while a convenient way to conceptualize teaching, is itself fraught with potential conflict, as while the Domains receive equal consideration, the realities of teaching can result in attention to one Domain adversely affecting or undermining another.

Emily's decision making is reflective also of Parker Palmer's (1998) belief that "good teaching comes from the identity and integrity of the teacher" (p. 10). For Emily, being a teacher necessitates accommodating the demands placed upon the teacher, whether the demands come from administrators, parents, or students. Thus, we see in Emily's narrative a juggling of sorts as she attempts to meet all of these demands and a glimpse of the integrity that motivates her actions.

Integrity, for Palmer (1998), means that the teacher must "discern what is integral to . . . selfhood, what fits and what does not." The teacher must "choose life-giving ways of relating to the forces that converge upon [him/her]" (p. 13). By choosing integrity, the teacher does not aspire for perfection; rather, he/she becomes "more real by acknowledging the whole of what [he/ or she] is" (p. 13). The actions that Emily relates demonstrate an understanding of who she is as teacher as well as a commitment to integrity. Her teacher identity is subsumed within the whole of who she is.

Additionally, Emily's commitment to innovative ways of teaching to meet the needs of all learners demonstrates another integral aspect of teaching identity. Emily is what Dewey (1977) calls an "educational pioneer" (p. 328). In her story, Emily refers to a "new activity" and "new learning opportunity," exemplifying Dewey's admonition that teachers must "think out of line with convention and custom" (p. 325), thus pointing to the importance of the teacher's imagination.

Nowhere in Danielson's domains do we find reference to "imagination," although perhaps implicit in Component 3c: Engaging Students in Learning is the need for the teacher to think imaginatively. Still, though, as Emily makes clear, the importance of the imagination and willingness to be an educational pioneer can be undermined by the nature of teaching in today's schools.

Furthermore, Emily demonstrates how reflection, a habit of mind, can aid novice teachers as they work to improve their expertise by making sense of their experiences. In retrospect, Emily's understanding of the value of careful planning and preparation (and having time to do so) was reinforced. At the same time, however, she began to understand the necessity to be flexible and to be able to adapt—not only in the classroom but outside it as well. A tension is thus exposed: the necessity of meticulous planning and preparation along-side the need to change if a situation calls for it. Additional reflection resulted in practical discoveries (how to meet parents' needs while still attending to planning and preparation) that can inform future decisions.

Emily's belief that teachers need to keep in mind the potential for unanticipated events and their often deleterious effects on teachers' efforts to plan, prepare, and implement is indicative of how experienced teachers think; they often have "theories of action," defined by McCutcheon (1992) as "sets of beliefs, images, and constructs" in place as a result of their practice (p. 191). Emily not only experienced how careful planning and preparation can be undermined by the vagaries of the school day but also went on to construct a theory of action for the future. She has discovered that the quirks of the "typical" school day necessitate the willingness and ability to create theories of action, a way of thinking that is perhaps especially important for teachers.

FOR DISCUSSION

1. Emily's story illustrates that teachers should be "educational pioneers." What will you do as a novice teacher to ensure that you will be an educational pioneer?
2. Create a scenario that you might experience as a teacher; for example, you have a carefully planned 40-minute lesson ready for your seniors for first period. However, during homeroom, the guidance counselor stops by to tell you that she must speak to your first period students for about 20 minutes about their college applications. Create a theory of action for this scenario.

FOR REFLECTION

Emily maintains that while teachers want to do "cool" things, this desire can "bump up against" the realities of teaching and the needs and demands of one's personal life. She asserts the need to "strike a balance." As a novice teacher, how might you strike a balance in your life that will allow you to meet the needs of your students, fulfill your desires to be an "educational pioneer," deal with the demands of the profession that extend beyond actual teaching, and allow you to live and enjoy your life outside of school?

FOR INQUIRY

1. Check teachers' schedules from a few secondary schools. How much preparation time is given to teachers on average? Is preparation time a

contractual item? Is preparation time built into the schedule of classes, or is it provided to teachers at the beginning or end of the school day? How does the amount of preparation time for secondary teachers compare with that of elementary teachers?

2. For some novice teachers, the challenges and demands of teaching become so overwhelming that they leave the profession. Conduct research that provides statistics related to teacher turnover and that share reasons for new teachers leaving the profession.

SUGGESTED READING

Cushman, K. (2005). *Fires in the bathroom: Advice for teachers from high school students*. New York: New Press.

Cushman, K. (2009). *Fires in the middle school bathroom: Advice for teachers from middle schoolers*. New York: New Press.

Goldstein, D. (2015). *The teacher wars: The history of America's most embattled profession*. New York: Anchor Books.

Palmer, P. (1998). *The courage to teach: Exploring the inner landscape of a teacher's life*. San Francisco: Jossey-Bass.

Simpson, D. J., Jackson, M. J. B., & Aycock, J. C. (2005). *John Dewey and the art of teaching: Toward reflective and imaginative practice*. Thousand Oaks, CA: Sage.

Wong, H., & Wong, R. (2009). *The first days of school: How to be an effective teacher*. Rev. ed. Mountain View, CA: Harry K. Wong.

Chapter Four

The Fault of Technology

When the Projector Dies

Alexander Hagood

Alex's narrative calls into question what teachers can and should do when the technology they have so painstakingly integrated into their lessons fails to work when they need it most.

In a world where technology has become prominent in the classroom, it is easy to become dependent on it; it also can become a major disruption when you find that it does not function properly. When this happens, entire lessons can be thrown off by the smallest problems and adjustments must be made on the spot.

I was setting up the classroom for the day, going over all of the little details to make sure that I was ready for class. Everything appeared to be in order. The warning bell rang and the students began to come in. I greeted them with a pleasant, "Good morning," as they finished conversations started in the hallways. I picked up the remote to start the projector, turning back to continue greeting the class. When several of the students were giving the SMART Board screen a weird look, I turned to the screen and my heart sank.

The late bell rang and I stood looking at a blue screen that was completely unusable. I could tell it was trying to recognize the screen that was meant to be projected, but something had gone wrong. I had a classroom of 25 students looking at me expectantly. I took a deep breath and took the step to call the technology department to have someone investigate the problem. However, I knew it would take them several minutes to arrive and at least another few minutes to determine the problem and fix it, a longer period of time than I could afford to lose. The students needed to be taught literature.

I looked around the room and noticed the chalkboard on the side of the room. It wasn't an ideal solution, but it had worked for teachers before. I had the students who sat closest to the chalkboard move to other locations in the room and shifted the desks out of my way. Rather than using the SMART Board, I made my charts on the chalkboard and had the students complete the discussions while I wrote their responses down with the chalk.

It seemed that I had the class back under control and things started going smoothly. However, it was not meant to last; the person from the technology department entered and started fiddling with the SMART Board projector. Students were starting to focus on what the tech guy was doing. This was tough to combat, but I used a few methods that seemed to work, including moving around the room when I could. This made it tougher for them to be unaccountable, since I was in close proximity rather than just the person at the chalkboard.

This day could have been a disaster. Many of the concepts I had planned to cover were literary skills that the students were expected to know by the end of the year. I was on a tight schedule, and this lesson going wrong could have totally thrown off my entire plan.

Looking back on this day made me realize that I made one big mistake. I planned everything that day around the assumption that the technology would work. I had not planned for any situation where the SMART Board would not be available to me. I quickly learned my lesson and in future lesson plans began working to figure out how I could accomplish the same objectives for the day if I found that some form of technology was not available to me.

There are many vagaries that we cannot ever prepare for. We can never predict when a school will go on lockdown due to a violent incident; we can never accurately predict when weather will get bad overnight and cancelling school the next day. But we can predict when technology can fail.

It is demonstrated every day that technology will not always work the way we intend it. We can ignore the possibility of it and hope for the best, as I did that day in the classroom, or we can prepare the adaptations portion of our lesson plan to include more than just how we can adjust the lesson to fit the individual needs of our students. Make notes about what you can do if any piece of technology goes down. Cover each technology you plan to use and make a plan for if it fails. It adds time to the planning process, but it saves time where it matters most, when we're standing in front of our students with the goal of engaging them in active learning.

Before reading Alex's reflection, think about how you would have handled this situation and what you might have done differently. Consider the following questions:

1. Do you think teachers are too dependent on technology for daily lessons? Should lesson plans always contain, as Alex suggests, adaptations in case technology fails?

2. Do you think all teachers should be technical experts when it comes to fixing glitches in their equipment? Should teachers have to go through additional training to be able to troubleshoot tech issues as they arise?

ALEX'S REFLECTION

After thinking about it again with Danielson's Framework in mind, I realize that my lesson, though planned out, still lacked the first two Domains: Planning and Preparation and Classroom Environment. My lesson was prepared, but it was only in a single format. Everything was dependent on the projector working. This lack of preparation showed as I stood in front of a class that was staring at me, waiting to hear what my plan was.

I had to admit to myself that I had no plan, and I couldn't wait for a person from technology to come; the lesson needed to move on. I lost several critical minutes in that day's lesson because I needed to process the events, take into account my objectives for the day, and determine how I could most effectively accomplish those goals without the technology that I had become so dependent on.

I managed to determine a method and lost more time having to shift my students around in order to have them appropriately situated so they could see the chalkboard I would be using in place of the projector and SMART Board. The lesson came to fruition, but I had to recover my own wits and recompose myself, since the incident shook my confidence.

The inclusion of the tech expert heavily affected the classroom environment because, despite my best efforts, I was already thrown off, which made me prone to further disruptions having a greater effect. I completed the lesson and accomplished my objectives, but not to the level I could have, had I been better prepared.

If I were to teach this lesson again, I would spend more time planning the lesson out; I would prepare for more potential situations. The lesson plan would not only include the primary plan but would have my backup plans: What will I do if the projector breaks? What will I do if I have to move students? What will I do if an administrator interrupts?

As a beginning teacher, these eventualities are not something I had thought of and, on that day, I wish I had. They will happen and there's really nothing we can do to avoid them. The only thing a teacher can do is to be prepared for as many situations as possible. At the time, the amount of planning I should have done evaded me. I heard the words in my studies and discussed ways that the concept could be implemented, but for me, it took the heat of the moment to drive the lesson home in a way that it never had been before.

This is a lesson that I have taken with me as I move forward in the field of teaching—plan, prepare, and expect the unexpected.

ALEX'S INTERVIEW WITH LINDA

I showed Alex the Danielson Domains with the detailed descriptors under each one, and asked my first question about which items specifically stood out to him from the general domains he'd selected. Alex focused on Component 1d: Demonstrating Knowledge of Resources under Domain 1: Planning and Preparation; he talked about resources including the technical personnel the school provided but stated that he wished he'd been able to think of an "on the spot" backup plan for his "old school" lack of technology. While he waited for a technician to arrive, he tried the on/off technique with the projection unit but didn't want to tinker with it further because he was not familiar with school equipment and he didn't want to damage anything.

He next pointed to the Classroom Environment Domain's components 2c: Managing Classroom Procedures and 2d: Managing Student Behavior, speaking specifically about losing instructional time and managing student behavior more effectively when his plan had to shift. Alex described that without a contingency plan, he resorted to moving his first-period students' desks away from the blackboard, causing loss of instructional time as well as increasing students' "chitchat" since they moved closer to their friends in relocating their desks.

Alex felt that having an alternative plan prior to that morning could have allowed him to move the students more effectively for management of the class time and the lesson. When asked about the other two domains, Alex responded that all of the domains do play important roles, but Domains 3 and 4 did not stand out specifically for him in this situation.

At one point Alex chastised himself about that lesson, stating that he "wasn't on top of things" and that he was "shaken in [his] pedagogical process." He remembered that he caught himself stumbling over his words more and said he felt a "visible shakenness" in this "unprepared moment." He claimed that he should have planned without the technology before teaching the lesson stating, "Technology will fail you when you most need it."

Alex also mused that he wished he'd asked himself before he'd taught that lesson questions like, "What will I do if technology is not available?" or "What if any of the pieces of technology fail in the lesson?" He went on to say that he'd wished he taken "even two more minutes" to think about where to place students and give clear directions of where to put them "to cause the least disruptive learning environment."

Upon further reflection, Alex stated that he would have begun the class immediately by explaining that he was having technical difficulties while directing students where to move their desks at the same time, saving minutes of instructional time. Alex said that he "stuck to the board" as a "safety zone" but wished he'd moved more in proximity to the students "to have better discussion."

LINDA'S COMMENTARY

Thinking like an expert in Alex's situation would require quick decision-making and efficient classroom management for three major events: 1) the projector failure, 2) moving students so writing could take place at the blackboard, and 3) the Instructional Technology (IT) person's interruption. When the SMART Board failed, Alex wrote that he "took a deep breath and took the step to call the technology department to have someone investigate the problem."

New teachers, especially student teachers as "guests" in a school, may hesitate to ask for help from or feel they even have time to get acquainted with the designated ITs in their buildings, and that is, if and when a school district can afford IT personnel and if there is one readily available when the problem occurs, since most school districts employ very few full-time tech support personnel.

As Sara Kajder (2010) states:

> There are teaching contexts rich with these kinds of supports: resource-rich classrooms or departments . . . instructionally minded technology support staff, . . . policies for bringing new tools and websites into classroom use. Across my work in multiple states, I have yet to see a context where all of these are in place. In some instances we luck out by finding three or more of these supports, and, in the majority, we are lucky to find one or two. (p. 104)

Furthermore, new teachers may not be aware that technical help is available or what kinds of support they may have access to, or they may not be willing or able to attend training sessions on the uses of the specific technology available in their school districts.

Direct access to technical support and time to learn newer technologies should be set aside for all teachers so that they can make the best use of technology for and with their students. In-service days before students return or early in the school year are probably the best times to teach new uses of equipment and troubleshooting for problems, especially in places where IT support is scarce.

Alex wrote that he "ignored the possibility" of the projector failing and took the chance that it would work when he needed it. Novice teachers may often prepare or feel they only have time to prepare a single way of lesson implementation.

Thinking more like an expert teacher would involve adapting the lesson plan to include how the class material and discussion could go smoothly without the SMART Board. Having a plan B, C, or D, for example, using the blackboard or having students use it, a handout, verbal discussion, or considerations of other forms of media-rich materials would have afforded Alex peace of mind that his lesson would go on without interruption, even if the technology part tanked. Expert teachers often switch to media-rich sources including photographs, magazines, print media, graphic novels, ads, construction paper and markers, and other high visuals for engagement when a tool like a SMART Board fails (e.g., Christel & Sullivan, 2007).

Another plan that may not work for every new teacher but which I have tried with some success on occasion is to ask a student who I have observed operate technology well to assist me for a very short time, either before class begins or during a very brief interruption of the lesson; our students are often more up-to-date and tech savvy than we are, and they may see something quite simple that is easily remedied that we cannot see.

Large group management must also always be a consideration for lesson engagement and less off-task behavior or "chitchat." Expertise with classroom management would have called for Alex to make sure that he had students' attention, that quick and effective directions were given for the change of seating arrangements, and that students were instructed not to move until all directions were clear. Higher student engagement at the blackboard where both he and the students wrote together, not just Alex doing all of the writing, might also have increased student engagement and could have allowed Alex to move around more, incorporating his suggestion of close proximity to students who were not actively engaged.

More active student engagement and a simple introduction of the IT person would probably have been an effective enough solution to the IT's disruption; we know that students are always curious when a visitor enters the classroom, so that is when an expert teacher should provide a short explanation for the visitor's presence and return quickly to the subject matter. The more time a new teacher takes to address the interruption or the visitor, the longer it will take to refocus students' attention to the lesson.

More important, Alex's narrative demonstrates that new teachers, as we learn in studies like the one conducted by Flanagan and Shottner (2016), may consider technology as having a "primary role" with the objectives of the lesson taking a secondary role, whereas experienced teachers tend to use technology as an "enhancement" to instruction, "preferring to use no technology 'if there was no clear or compelling reason to use it.'" Incorporating technology into a lesson plan, for example, using a SMART Board, is only as good as the technology functioning properly; the SMART Board can never be the replacement, only the vehicle, for a strong, successful lesson plan.

Flanagan and Shottner (2016) also make a key discovery in their study of Kathy, an experienced teacher, and Susan, a beginning teacher, regarding how much status a teacher has with students and how technology may be used more effectively with more teaching experience that we can apply appropriately to Alex's situation as well:

> Teaching experience may indeed lead to better or more effective uses of technology during instruction, independent of a teacher's experiences with a specific technology (Hughes, 2005; Ruthven, Hennessy, & Brindley, 2004). For example, Kathy's status as an experienced teacher may have supported more effective instruction, regardless of whether technology was used, while Susan's status as a novice teacher may have influenced her students' off-task behavior when transitioning between or using technology. (para. 71)

We know, as Alex testifies, that his students became more talkative and off-topic when the technology failed, and his sudden lack of confidence as a student teacher in knowing how to handle the situation readily and competently could easily have influenced the students' unfocused behavior. Alex's narrative reminds us that technology can be unreliable and a source of frustration at the most inopportune times, but we also know how important it is in today's classrooms, and in the end, the benefits clearly outweigh the risks for use.

As supported in the Flanagan and Shottner (2016) article,

> Technology offers a means to differentiate instruction, motivate students, improve instruction, provide visual cues, and improve learning, especially in the area of literacy (O'Neil & Perez, 2003; Shoffner, de Oliveira & Angus, 2010; Sternberg et al., 2007). Additionally, technology has a potentially positive impact on secondary ELA instruction when used in and selected appropriately for classroom learning (Swenson, 2006). The International Society for Technology in Education (ISTE, 2008) promoted the use of technology in instruction to customize students' learning experiences and provide a variety of instructional methods. NCTE (2010) echoed these benefits while emphasizing the importance of using technology to prepare students for postschool outcomes. (para. 63)

Alex's narrative helps us to remember that we absolutely should use and keep current with the technology resources we have at our fingertips, but we must also remember to make a contingency plan (or several) if the computer, pro-jector, website, media, or other tech tools at our disposal crash unexpectedly.

FOR DISCUSSION

1. How does Alex's narrative show that teaching is a complex set of spon-taneous decisions?
2. According to Flanagan and Shoffner (2016), "English teachers must de-velop a level of technological skill that supports their usage of technology and their incorporation of technology in English instruction" (para. 12). Do you agree or disagree with this statement? How does this statement apply in Alex's case?

FOR REFLECTION

Alex stated that this incident "shook his confidence." What suggestions would you have for Alex to help him act more calmly and in control when the lesson did not go as he'd planned? What techniques do you know or would you like to learn to become more like an expert teacher with regard to build-ing your confidence in your classroom?

FOR INQUIRY

1. Consider the benefits of and challenges to technology use. Keep track of how many times per week you depend on technology to assist you in your classroom. Make a log of how well you felt the lesson went because of the incorporation of your technical resources and how many times the technol-ogy did not go as you had planned. See if you can write the same lesson plan at least once a week without the use of any digital or online resources to help you and how your thinking changes about the lesson plan when you adapt for low or no tech.
2. Which hard copy or online texts have been most helpful to you in terms of using technology in your classroom? Are there any texts you would highly recommend to other teachers that incorporate uses of technology with the subject matter?

SUGGESTED READING

Christel, M. T., & Sullivan, S. (Eds.). (2007). *Lesson plans for creating media-rich classrooms*. Urbana, IL: NCTE.

Kajder, S. (2010). *Adolescents and digital literacies*. Urbana: NCTE.

Welcome to teaching English with technology. (2015). EdTechTeacher, Inc. Retrieved from http://tewt.org/.

Part II

THE CLASSROOM ENVIRONMENT

The Classroom Environment takes into account the classroom as a community with emphasis on rapport and respect among all members. Subsumed within this domain are also classroom and student management, the establishment of classroom procedures, and the organization of physical space.

Chapter Five

Creating an Atmosphere of Respect and Rapport

Scott Gibbons

In this chapter, Scott shares his beliefs about the importance of rapport with students—rapport that ensures that students will perform well in his class. For Scott, good teaching means caring about students.

"Let me know if you need to talk" is often enough to establish rapport with a student.

One of my students missed several days of school because she was in the hospital and was later diagnosed with diabetes. When she returned, I told her that I had many students over the years who had been diagnosed with the disease and that they were doing great in college while still maintaining their health. Then I compared her need for regular medication to my need to take oral enzymes because I have cystic fibrosis. This information was exchanged during a five-minute conversation before class started. It did not take long for her to open up to me about her struggles with and fears about the disease. She was already a strong student, but after our talk, she excelled in my class.

Another way that I build and maintain rapport with my students is by respecting what they share in class. During discussions, I build on responses students give, even if they are off the mark; I use their comments to develop ideas that somehow relate to what we're discussing or to the lesson or unit. As a result of my efforts to validate and affirm students' responses, they feel that their contributions are valuable.

When students have a good rapport with their teachers, they want to perform well. When I have failed to develop a good relationship with a student, that student often struggles and never asks for help. But the students who are always e-mailing me and asking me questions are the students who get the most out of my class. If a student is afraid to ask questions, it is not the student's fault; it is my fault. I have not made him/her feel as if his/her ideas are important, and I have not made him/her feel comfortable enough take risks, to be vulnerable.

I have come to realize that creating rapport with students is just as important as content knowledge, experience, and organization. I have also come to realize that rapport is created by different means and at a different rate with each student. A student who refuses to speak within the first few months of class may become the most talkative student by the end of the semester. But some students open up right away.

A teacher's pedagogical skills are useless if he is unable to create a rapport with students.

Take a moment to consider any questions that you have about Scott's thoughts about rapport. Do you have any concerns about creating rapport with students? With creating an environment of respect and rapport?

SCOTT'S REFLECTION

Thinking about my reflection and examples from my own teaching with Danielson's Framework in mind, I realize that several of Danielson's domains are represented and that much of what I do both in the classroom and outside of the classroom is developed naturally by sticking to some simple principles: give respect to earn it and live your content so that students develop a vested interest.

Regarding Domain 2, I believe a good rapport with students makes a teacher better prepared to manage any potential discipline issues. I have few discipline problems in my classroom, in part because my students know that I care about them and that I care about the job that I am doing. If I put in the effort to develop a relationship with each of them, and I make connections with them and the content, then they have no reason to object to any classroom procedures or assignments because they are aware that each assignment or procedure has their best interests in mind, even if it isn't immediately apparent to them. Rarely do my students object to any classwork, nor do they ask, "Why are we doing this?" because they are already aware of the goal.

Also included in Domain 2 is the arrangement of the classroom; I have made my classroom environment welcoming—with warm lighting and comfortable seating, which tends to open students up to taking risks.

Because students feel safe in my classroom, they are more willing to take risks in discussions and their writing. They are aware that I am there to support them, so their mentality becomes a "Why not try?" mentality. This connects to Domain 3 because my instruction is planned with my students in mind. If I did not know anything about my students, then I would not be able to relate the material to them, which would create a gap between what I want them to learn and how they learn.

Developing a working relationship with students also helps me to be flexible with students who require more time and guidance and stricter with students who need to be pushed. Without knowledge and understanding of each student, I would not be able to derive from them their best work.

Reflecting on my own teaching and comparing it to the teaching of colleagues whom I've observed, I can see that many teachers struggle when it comes to rapport with students. This struggle might have something to do with a lack of reflection on the teacher's part. I daily note what worked well and what didn't. I note information I gained about students, and I note struggles and strengths of students. This habit helps me create and maintain rapport with my students while also informing my teaching.

Although it is difficult to take the time to note and reflect each day, without these habits, all of the day's information tends to slip away. As indicated in Domain 4, reflection is one of the major components of strong teaching.

SCOTT'S INTERVIEW WITH JO-ANNE

In an e-mail, Scott shared the rethinking that emerged when he thought about what he had written about rapport with students and how his thinking about this aspect of teaching relates to Danielson's domains.

While rapport is a component of Domain 2, Scott made the connection to Component 1b, writing that "it makes me think about the times when I've adjusted my curriculum based upon what I have learned about students' heritage." Having made the effort to speak with a few Hispanic students about their family backgrounds, he then incorporated some Hispanic short stories into a few literature units. To help students understand themes related to magical realism in short stories and excerpts from novels, he invited his Hispanic students to describe their lives in Mexico. He believes that all students were more engaged in the unit as a result of his efforts.

Scott also made the point that his classes in which Hispanic students were enrolled were a bit different from his other classes, although the objectives for all students were the same. How those objectives were met, though, was different among his classes.

Furthermore, Scott noted that his efforts to learn more about his Hispanic students were possible only because he had established a rapport with them.

He saw this as relating to Component 1d, as he believed that "I had to have an understanding of my resources in order to make that lesson happen." He also perceived a connection to Component 3e "because I always look for reasons and ideas to adjust my lessons and units." Scott believes that if a unit is more relevant to students' lives and experiences, then interest is piqued and learning occurs.

When Scott was prompted to share questions that arose from reexamining his narrative and reflection, he extended his focus on rapport between teacher and students to rapport among students, stating that "I want to figure out ways to help students develop a . . . rapport with each other." He sees this as an equally important part of classroom environment that goes beyond merely providing "getting to know you" activities. He wants students to develop a "deeper working rapport with one another" so that collaborative work will be easier and more productive. He asked himself, "What are some ways to make students as comfortable with each other as they are with me?"

Scott embedded an anecdote within his piece about rapport concerning a student diagnosed with diabetes. When he was asked to think again about this student and how he had made a point to connect and empathize with her, he recalled a graduate course he had taken for which he had created a private blog for five students with very different disabilities in which they anonymously responded to his questions and then carried on a discussion with each other using these responses.

He wrote that all of these students spoke to him about how helpful it was for them to learn that there were other students in his classes who were "just like them." Scott wrote that their conversations "blossomed" and to the point that they did not need him to prompt them to discuss how their disabilities affected their school life.

Scott ended his interview by returning to the importance of rapport and its connection to effective teaching and learning. Essentially, rapport means caring about students. Scott believes that his students do well "because I care."

JO-ANNE'S COMMENTARY

Scott's focus on and belief in the importance of rapport reflects Domain 2: Classroom Environment, Component 2a: Creating an Environment of Respect and Rapport, yet, for Scott, rapport is subsumed within Domain 1: Planning and Preparation and Domain 3: Instruction. He maintains, for instance, that finding out a bit about students' backgrounds and family histories allowed him to create an effective lesson—not only for his Hispanic students but for all of his students. He also perceived this effort as responsive teaching (Component 3e).

While Danielson's domains are discrete elements of a framework for teaching, teaching is more organic than the framework suggests. Teaching is, in fact, a complex endeavor, qualifying as a complex system; that is, composed of many parts that interconnect in intricate ways. For Scott, delving into students' family histories and backgrounds, a process of building rapport, also informed planning and preparation and instruction. Thus, one part of effective teaching, creating an environment of respect and rapport, has consequences for teachers' planning and preparation and instruction. The key role of rapport in teaching, then, is highlighted, as well as the complexities inherent in the act of teaching.

Scott also sees rapport among students as important to teaching and learning. He wants to help students develop good working relationships, seeing these relationships as essential for effective collaborative work. This goal, fostering rapport among students, suggests that Scott sees his classroom as a community. Burden (2012, p. 8) refers to Sapon-Shevin's (2010) characteristics of learning communities, including "mutual liking" that results when students are encouraged to "know and like their classmates." Burden also states that teachers often use collaborative learning activities to help create and maintain learning communities (p. 9).

Included with efforts to establish rapport is caring. Scott attributes his students' successes to the fact that he cares. Drawing on Nel Noddings's (1992) work, Danielwicz (2001) defines caring as a "reciprocal relation between people" (p. 165). "Reciprocal" is a key word, as Noddings asserts that when a teacher demonstrates care for a student, the student must acknowledge this care.

When Scott demonstrated his concern for his student who had diabetes, making a point to reach out to her, his efforts were acknowledged; furthermore, this student did even better in his class than she had before. A quick, five-minute conversation, during which Scott demonstrated caring and empathy for a student, affected this student's performance in his class, evidence, again, of the primary role that rapport can take in teaching.

Danielwicz (2001) also notes that caring teachers are attentive and persistent, and she states that she is "vigilantly mindful . . . watching and listening for those details that reveal the individual student's particular concerns, interests, and inclinations" (p. 166). We see, certainly, attentiveness displayed in his anecdote, attentiveness that resulted in his ability to sense his student's concerns.

Thus, Scott's belief that his students do well because he cares is no doubt a valid contention, along with his belief that sound pedagogy must be augmented by efforts to build rapport and caring relationships with students.

Creating and maintaining rapport, though, is not necessarily easy and it can be fraught with challenges to teachers' roles as professionals. Preservice and novice teachers are often advised to be "friendly" with their students but to avoid being their students' "friends." But this is somewhat facile advice, as how do teachers maintain friendliness while avoiding being perceived as a student's friend?

In Scott's case, the conversation with the student with diabetes and his asking his Hispanic students about their home lives and heritages were motivated by his goal to help these students as learners. Understanding how a disease like diabetes can affect a student's performance and learning and likewise understanding that students tend to be more engaged when lessons are relevant to their own lives and experiences led Scott to reach out to these students. While his efforts were certainly indicative of friendliness, showing empathy, interest, and concern, his intentions were driven by understanding of pedagogy, and his behavior demonstrated integrity and ethical conduct (Component 4f).

Furthermore, his decision to share with his student that he has cystic fibrosis resulted from his efforts to convey empathy and thus was also an ethical action. Teachers' decisions to share their personal lives must be made carefully, with attention paid to reasons for sharing and what consequences may result.

Finally, another aspect of Scott's commentary is also noteworthy—his habit of noting and reflecting at the end of each school day. He believes that this habit informs his teaching, and, of course, reflecting on teaching is a component of Domain 4: Professional Responsibilities. Scott's notes fulfill a practical function; they help him remember pertinent information.

However, these notes also serve a kind of tool for developing personal theories of teaching. Gere, Fairbanks, Roop, and Schaafsma (1992) state that teachers must reflect on teaching practices in a quest to "continually change and improve . . . theory" (p. 60). While teachers use theory to inform and guide their practice, reflecting on their practice provides opportunity to generate theory as well—a theory-into-practice-into-theory process.

Teaching thus becomes a creative act, with teachers agents of their own change and improvement. Scott's notes about what worked and what didn't may guide future teaching; however, they also may help him fashion a personal theory and a consistent way of thinking about the act of teaching that will help him adhere to his beliefs about what effective teaching entails.

FOR DISCUSSION

1. What are some ways that you will use to help you create and maintain an environment or respect and rapport when you have your own classroom?

2. What connections do you see between creating an atmosphere of respect and rapport and managing student behavior, another component of Domain 2?

FOR REFLECTION

Parker Palmer (1998) writes, "Good teachers possess a capacity for connectedness. They are able to weave a complex web of connections among themselves, their subject, and their students so that they can learn to weave a world for themselves" (p. 11). How does this characterization of "good teachers" influence and expand your understanding of what good teaching entails?

FOR INQUIRY

One of Scott's students was diagnosed with diabetes, and Scott made a point to reach out to her in an effort to allay her concerns about her health and the effects of this condition of her life. What policies and procedures do schools follow when students are diagnosed with serious illnesses? How are teachers informed? What role does the school nurse play? What accommodations are teachers asked to make? What criteria are used to determine if the accommodations asked for are reasonable and within a teacher's capabilities? What recourse does a teacher have if he believes that he is putting himself in professional jeopardy by agreeing to intervene if a student needs assistance?

SUGGESTED READING

Noddings, N. (1992). *The challenge to care in schools: An alternative approach to education*. New York: Teachers College Press.

Palmer, Parker. (1998). *The courage to teach: Exploring the inner landscape of a teacher's life*. San Francisco: Jossey-Bass.

Chapter Six

Many Things to Many People

Life as a New Teacher

Heather Lowry

Heather's narrative describes the unique challenges she faced in two teaching positions she accepted over two years in two states with very different students and families.

My first full-time teaching job in an urban setting in Maryland was very opposite to most of my educational experiences; it was in a high-need school district that paid well and was intentionally searching for out-of-state certified teachers. The interview process (I knew no one and nothing about the school district), was very simple; the benefits that came with accepting a job in this school were terrific. Although farther from my home than I originally wanted, I packed and moved south to begin my official teaching career with a spring in my step and a wealth of knowledge that I was sure would coast me through whatever was waiting for me in my future seventh-grade classroom.

My first surprise as a new full-time teacher was that I wasn't just going to be teaching seventh-grade language arts but also seventh-grade social studies, specifically geography. I was confident in my teaching ability but not so confident in my geography knowledge, so I read up on strategies for teaching geography and tried my best to be as polished and prepared as possible for that first day of school.

My students were unlike any other group I'd ever encountered. From low socioeconomic backgrounds, with broken homes and often unsafe or unstable living conditions, some of my students were homeless and moved from school to school. Many had behavioral challenges, and not the behavioral challenges that I'd become accustomed to from my student teaching or substitute teaching experiences.

These were extremely volatile, engrained behavioral issues. Students were exposed to very adult issues at very early ages and were forced to deal with problems that were well above their maturity levels. Uninterested in school, probably because they found it difficult to trust authority or adults, they were not usually eager to learn. Many of them showed up just so they would be guaranteed at least two meals that day, breakfast and lunch; dinner at home was never promised.

My teaching became almost entirely about relationship building, quick thinking, flexibility, and compassion, and less about constructing perfect sentences and knowing where the Nile River is located. I had to let go of my duty to push the learning objective for that particular day and embrace my duty to be a consistent, positive, and understanding role model for these students, using my content area as a way to enhance their experience, not as the guiding factor.

Often I was challenged, cursed at, books were thrown across the room, chairs and desks were upset, and lockers/walls/and sometimes even other students, were punched. I had to navigate intense bullying situations that stretched far beyond quiet snickers or whispered unkind comments. I had moments of questioning my decision to enter education. Most days, it was just me and 31 students, nearly half of those who had specialized behavioral or educational plans attached to them, alone in a room for an hour and a half. I had to make sure that not only were they learning, but that they, and I, were, first and foremost, safe and comfortable.

Keeping all of my students sitting still in a seat each block period was unrealistic and mostly impossible, so I quickly embraced movement and "controlled chaos" in tandem with my teaching. I had to "let go" of some sense of "control" that I'd come to understand from my own schooling experiences and learn to be comfortable with these changes to accomplish a larger goal. I had to establish routine upon routine so that they were always busy and always focused, even if it was simply passing out papers to their fellow students or making sure their area was clean and organized after each activity. I put in place many proactive behavioral systems so that students were constantly working toward a behavioral goal and ultimately, a reward, if they met the expectation.

My primary goal every day, no matter what situations I faced, was to be kind and compassionate to these students. I had to earn their respect and their trust every single day; that was the only factor that kept them listening to me, kept them from lashing out at me or their peers, and showing up for class, handing in assignments, and participating when I asked. They knew I cared about them and their success, and for most of them, that eventually meant that they started to care, too.

My colleagues at this school were some of the best I have ever worked with. We dealt with challenges that many teachers don't ever have to face.

We were given some of the best professional development available and plenty of beneficial in-service trainings. We had grade level team meetings, subject level team meetings, team planning and cross-curricular objectives on a weekly basis. We shared lesson plans, resources, and worked together constantly for both content and student success. I had iPad carts and technology trainings that helped to make the instructional part of my job much easier and more accessible for my challenging audience.

Parental involvement at this school was, not surprisingly, rather low. There were many parents who did not know what their child's grades were, what classes he/she took, or how to find out. Many of these families simply didn't or couldn't care because of extraneous circumstances.

The administration did an excellent job of going out of their way to make conferences with parents and provide them with ways of having complete access to their child's teachers and grades. They worked tirelessly on student and family engagement, constantly attempting to build relationships with families and students to alleviate behavioral issues and solve problems outside of the classrooms; it was encouraging to know that their support was always a phone call or room away.

I experienced a deep sense of loss that I had to leave behind the students and colleagues who, through the challenges we faced together, felt more like family than like work. I was fortunate to leave knowing that I had impacted lives in a deep and real way, and admittedly, mostly my own.

I was newly engaged, and my future husband's business led me back north to Ohio. Although I would miss a lot about my old position, I self-admittedly was looking forward to leaving behind the serious behavioral challenges so that I could focus more on the teaching and less on the behavior management in my next role. What I didn't anticipate was that once again I would have to balance teaching with other obligations that would be just as challenging.

My new position was teaching ninth-grade English, yearbook class, and running the Rotary-Interact Club. I was taking on a high school position in a much smaller, more rural school district, very much like the one I had grown up in and had been used to all my life. The comfort level was an easier adjustment—another supportive administration and hard-working colleagues.

I was the only ninth grade English teacher in the district, and therefore, was an island for creating curriculum. My colleagues, all talented and most of whom were veteran teachers, worked very independently of one another; their content was solely their own. I worked as much as possible with the other grade level English teachers to establish my curriculum when we had the opportunities during in-service and prep periods; but ultimately, the choices and the implementation of the standards were mine alone. There wasn't time set aside in planning to meet with other teachers unless you sought it out yourself. Although I felt totally confident as a behavior manager, in this role my confidence really grew as an instructor of my content.

My students came from middle-to-upper-class rural families, mostly white, most of which already valued education. Students were groomed with a strong sense of volunteerism and educational drive. It was a huge surprise to me that when I held my first informational Rotary Club meeting, I had more than one hundred students joining this community-service based club, in addition to everything else they did. The club itself was demanding in its requirements for time commitment, but students came out in droves just to be part of giving back and building their resumes.

To teach these kids would be a cakewalk compared to my last experience, I thought; these students were already interested and driven by learning. They weren't facing the types of challenges that my seventh grade urban population unfortunately had to face; their focus could be about their academic pursuits and success instead of sheer survival. I realized quickly that I would be much more than just "teaching"—I would be running organizations that were completely separate from the learning, and I was going to have to balance all those roles at once.

My role at this school became less about being a consistent, safe place provider for my students and more of college-and-career mentor to help them achieve their aspirations after high school. Although this did include strong instruction in English, it equally included my heavy involvement in extracurricular activities at the school, some that were not compensated for. I volunteered for a plethora of activities and causes, even assisting a weightlifting club after school in addition to my paid extracurriculars and my teaching duties. In this district, that was the way to best build relationships with the students and with the community.

I still served as a role model for these students, but in a more academic-focused and citizenship-based way. These students were looking to me as an educator and a mentor, and not as "parent." They already had that role filled, and it was highly likely that whoever their parent was would be e-mailing or calling me regularly to keep up with their progress.

The parents, like the community, were highly involved in school activities, something that I also had to get used to. I had constant e-mail communication about assignments, student progress, and grades from very interested parents. My prep periods were as filled with fielding requests from parents and community obligations as they were about preparing for what I was going to teach later that week. Sundays quickly became monopolized by lesson planning and material making so that my planning and teaching materials were ready to go for the week ahead. My students and their success came first, which meant my teaching first and foremost, but that included making sure my extracurricular duties were excelling.

Yearbook advising, including managing the budget of the entire high school's yearbook, was a large chunk of my time. I was lucky enough to be given a class period for yearbook every day, but the duties of this role far extended the time period that was set aside. This was like running a mini-business with employees who required from me extensive training in design, marketing, budgeting and finance, and advertising skills.

Time management was the name of the game in this teaching role. My behavioral challenges were at zero, especially when I compared this group of students to my previous experience. I was still, at the core, a relationship-based teacher, but these students needed and respected a different type of relationship; they wanted to respect you for your abilities, accomplishments, and involvement in their success.

Quite honestly, I had anticipated being in this district for the majority of my teaching career. However, after my husband and I got married, we were fortunate to receive an opportunity through his business to move back to my hometown. I was thrilled to be moving "home" near my family again, but bittersweet to yet again have to give up a teaching role that I very much enjoyed and a population of students that I had, again, truly cared about.

Much like when I left my first teaching position, I missed the sense of community that this role had brought me. My administration, my colleagues, the parents, and the students were all intricately involved with one another; there was a sense of camaraderie as a member of the community that was second to none. Although it was a time commitment challenge from start to finish, there are few times I've felt as rewarded as when, after I moved away, the district mailed me a copy of the yearbook that my students completed under my supervision, the tangible results of the effect I'd had on my students and the school community itself.

Both of my teaching experiences brought out aspects of my pedagogy that I had never been quite prepared for. You aren't ever prepared to teach an entirely different subject days before the school year begins. You aren't told what to do when your student is homeless and has absolutely no interest in school, much less any opportunity to even consider doing homework. You aren't told what to do when you are asked to run a mini-business, with a small group of high school students as your employees, in addition to your already challenging task of teaching the subject you were hired to teach. You aren't prepared to be asked to be all things at all times to the students that count on you and the people that have entrusted you with their care.

You learn on-the-job; you will become flexible in both your thought process and your teaching style because you have to be. Sometimes you're a parent, sometimes you're a community servant, sometimes you're running a business, and sometimes you're simply trying to make it through the day without giving up.

In my Maryland role, one of my most rewarding moments was when a student who previously fast-pitched a copy of his book across my classroom in anger and walked out of the room later told me that the very book he had thrown was now the first book he'd ever read front-to-back, and that he actually enjoyed. He started to raise his hand during discussions and completed the assignments we worked on. He said he was interested in continuing to read because "Some books ain't so bad" after all.

Equally as powerful, in my Ohio position, one of my senior yearbook students asked me to accompany her to her "Top 10" recognition dinner—an evening dedicated to the top ten seniors where they can bring one teacher who impacted them the most. She gave a speech about how I affected her, and I, in turn, got to do the same for her.

Those are snapshots of the moments that remind me why I'll probably always be a teacher, and why my work, no matter what it is that I am asked to do, is meaningful and relevant. Being a teacher means you are supernatural, ever-evolving, and able to accomplish anything if you're dedicated to what you do and who you're doing it for.

Before reading Heather's reflection, think about the following questions:

1. Considering what you know thus far about the teaching profession, which of Heather's two teaching positions would present the most challenges for you and why?
2. How would you handle an angry student who throws a book or upsets a desk in your classroom? How would you communicate with a parent who is constantly e-mailing you about her or his child's grades?

HEATHER'S REFLECTION

Each of Danielson's Domains highlight the many hats I am required to wear as an educator, and how it is essential to "be prepared to be unprepared"—especially as a new hire in a full-time position. Pre-service teachers often focus on the curriculum and instruction aspects of teaching (Domains 1 and 3). It's easy to gloss over Domains 2 and 4 (and more specifically each detail in each domain) when you don't have your own classroom.

When it becomes your own, those Domains take on much more significant value and are equally as important as the planning you do or the ways in which you instruct your content. The biggest realizations I came to were that 1) Domains 2 and 4 were so much more a part of my every day teaching life and responsibilities than I ever originally imagined before I was hired as a full-time teacher, and 2) the details of each of these domains are not fully understood or realized until you create your own meaning and relevancy for them through your own experiences on the job.

Specifically during my time as a seventh-grade teacher in an urban school setting, Domain 2: Classroom Environment, became foremost to being successful in any other Danielson Domain; if my students didn't feel safe or comfortable, or recognize that their presence was valued and vital to the success of the rest of the class, then no learning could ever occur.

No matter how sharp my instructional delivery or how prepared I was to instruct, students would have taken nothing away if I hadn't focused on comfort, agency, and safety from the harsh realities of their outside worlds. My "battle" every day was to ensure that I was doing everything I could to provide the type of environment that this at-risk population of students could identify with and feel supported within. Planning and Preparation became more about preparing the environment or the conditions of the instruction, not the instruction itself. If the students didn't feel respected, safe, or welcomed by me and by their peers in the room, they were not going to succeed.

During my time as a ninth-grade English teacher, yearbook adviser, and Rotary-Interact Club adviser, I was confronted daily with the demands of Domain 4: Professional Responsibilities, which I discovered are so much more than just showing up each day being a professionally dressed, upstanding member of the school community. I was much more than just an educator—I was a businesswoman, a community servant, an event planner, an accountant, and a marketing guru. I was many things in addition to "teacher" in order to be successful.

"Professional responsibilities" took on a much more concrete meaning when I was required to give just as much of my time to outside-the-classroom activities as I was my instruction of English. Domain 4d: Participating in the Professional Community, is very general and doesn't quite articulate how many different roles we have to take on; this one aspect of one Domain is both very time-consuming and also critical to your success in your school and community.

It was not possible for me to understand just how deeply Classroom Environment and Professional Responsibilities would impact my job until I had to navigate those waters. It was also not clear how Domains 1 and 2 could shift or change in accordance to the other Domains, that is, how your planning can be directed toward the safety of your students or the behaviors that you are trying to control just as much as it can be about what is happening in your lesson plan.

It is difficult to emulate the types of decisions you'll have to make when you have your own classroom and are solely responsible for roles within your school community. Using Danielson as a guide, it becomes your responsibility to fill in the gaps for which parts of her Framework you didn't anticipate beforehand or the meanings you'll need to reconstruct in order to fit your situation. Teaching is an extremely fluid career, and though these domains serve as a roadmap for us as educators, you are ultimately responsible for where you end up and how to get there for the best interests of your students and the roles that you are entrusted to fill.

HEATHER'S INTERVIEW WITH LINDA

Regarding her first position in Maryland, Heather explained that Domain 2, Component 2a: Creating an Environment of Respect and Rapport: was her top priority. This component was "paramount," she said, or "nothing would get done." With 22 to 32 students from various backgrounds, she needed to offer equitable learning opportunities for each person, and she had to establish clear standards of conduct and behavioral expectations with consequences while being both kind and flexible—not an easy task for any teacher. She set standards and followed the school's discipline code, keeping track of any students who had five or more infractions.

Creating a system of "table points" fashioned after "the tribes on the *Survivor* television show," she stated, teams of students received plus or minus points daily and could earn weekly rewards like food or no homework if they earned the most plus points as a table. This strategy promoted not only appropriate behaviors but also built a sense of community among the students. She consistently modeled appropriate interactions and respectful behaviors; she described herself as "approachable" to her students.

Heather told me that as a Master's in Teaching English graduate, she would not have been as hesitant to move south and take a "not ideal" half-time social studies position after learning so much from this experience. She was grateful for the professional development, team teaching, and lesson design training she received even before she started the school year. She explained that the "environment affects your planning." She learned to work collaboratively as a team; she added that teaching in blocks of ninety minutes became easier as she established rapport with her students, and she learned to "never finish early" and "always have a backup plan."

In Ohio, Heather was amazed at the many different hats she was required to wear; she said she became "highly valued" because she did "things others [the more seasoned teachers] didn't want to do." Extracurricular activities were important to these students; academics and outside activities were "very equal there." Heather appreciated that she had more autonomy in this second position, but because of the high involvement of parental support and interest, she also felt the pressure of some parents who sent constant e-mails checking up on their children's progress.

Much of Heather's second job centered around ethical behavior and Domain 4: Professional Responsibilities, especially Components 4 b, c, and d in maintaining accurate records, communicating with families, and participating in school service and events; she had to have a solid knowledge of school regulations, and unlike her first position, a direct, constant line with families was a definite priority.

Going back to Domain 1: Planning and Preparation, Heather explained that although the maturity levels of her ninth graders varied, she felt she became "a better teacher" here; she always had to know her material for her 40-minute classes because students were generally better behaved, better readers, and better at following her expectations more precisely.

She also felt "relaxed a little more" with these students and told me that she could have "conversations" in her classes that allowed her more freedom, improvisation, and flexibility. In concluding our interview, Heather added that she'd wished she had more time to get to know both schools and that one thing both had in common was that it was "rare that her daily plan was exact" in either situation.

LINDA'S COMMENTARY

Any new teaching position, and particularly the first teaching job, always requires navigating much unchartered territory. New teachers in our state, Pennsylvania, often have to apply for their first full-time teaching job out of state, frequently in urban areas where demand is higher and the students are considered more at-risk. Our English education program advocates that teacher candidates have a range of field experiences before they begin their first year of employment. Some candidates are able to observe and to pre-student teach first-hand at urban schools in Philadelphia, Johnstown, and Pittsburgh, where others, due to transportation, economic, or other factors, may need to do their practicum closer to our rural university and their suburban or rural homes.

For some, like Heather, a first teaching job in an unfamiliar surrounding can be an unanticipated cultural, geographical, and social awakening. Her students represented different cultures, socioeconomic classes, and many had special needs. She worked in a district with little parental involvement, and some students were homeless. Heather was fortunate to be hired in a school district that believed in team training and mentored her through her first year with many in-service and professional development opportunities. Even so, she felt underprepared to deal with some discipline and management issues she faced on a daily basis with large classes and long class periods. And she was hired to teach two subjects, one she had never taught before.

As a new master's degree graduate, curriculum was not the difficult part for Heather. Getting students to trust and to respect her so learning could occur was her challenge. She could not accomplish the goals for the lesson if she could not establish rapport. Heather, thinking like an experienced teacher, developed routines and taught from bell to bell, setting high expectations, and wasting little to no class time. She consistently modeled appropriate behaviors and rewarded students in their teams when they exhibited positive interactions.

"They knew I cared about them and their success, and for most of them—most of the time—that eventually meant that they started to care, too." As Nel Noddings, Jacks Professor Emerita of Child Education at Stanford University advocates, exercising an ethic of mutual caring, closely aligned with promoting social justice for all students, is one of the ways teachers build and maintain respect and rapport:

> The key, central to care theory, is this: caring-about (or, perhaps a sense of justice) must be seen as instrumental in establishing the conditions under which caring-for can flourish. Although the preferred form of caring is cared-for, caring-about can help in establishing, maintaining, and enhancing it. Those who care about others in the justice sense must keep in mind that the objective is to ensure that caring actually occurs. Caring-about is empty if it does not culminate in caring relations. (Noddings, 2002: 23–24, cited in M. Smith, 2016, para. 10)

In her second year in more rural Ohio, Heather faced a new set of issues. She was required to spend hours as a business manager, organizer, social director, and publisher. She had to deal with high accountability placed on her by the parents and the community. Usually the newest, most inexperienced hires are the ones who are asked or required to do, frequently without extra pay, the above-and-beyond duties the seasoned faculty have already taken their turns doing.

Newer teachers have to negotiate extra duties in their early years so as not to burn out from the overload of teaching and non-academic responsibilities. One way to avoid the wearing-too-many-hats dilemma is, as in Heather's case, to receive an assignment such as the yearbook as a class period rather than as an extracurricular activity.

Another is to suggest in the employment interview one or two additional talents or skills you would consider as side contracts including coaching a sport or directing the school musical, for example. Heather's narrative reminds us that every teaching situation is different, that the university clinical experiences may or may not match the reality of the first job, and that we have to be ready for the unexpected.

FOR DISCUSSION

1. Classroom environment plays a key role in student learning. Consider what Heather did to make her classroom a safe and productive learning space. What additional steps to create a positive space would you take if this was your first position?
2. How will you manage the different hats you'll be required to wear when you are a beginning teacher? What organizational methods will you employ to balance both your teaching load and also extracurricular responsibilities you may be asked to undertake?

FOR REFLECTION

Heather states that her first job teaching seventh grade English and geography seemed "not ideal"; later, she reflects that she learned so much from it. What would be your ideal teaching job, and why would this situation be your top choice? How likely do you think you are to receive this ideal position, and what will it take to achieve it? Can you describe a teaching situation that was not so ideal for you, but where you learned more than you expected?

FOR INQUIRY

1. Conduct an online search of at least two school districts' websites where you are likely to apply for a teaching position. How do the two school websites compare in terms of mission, goals, size, student population, activities and events, and community involvement? Which school appeals to you more and why?

2. Research how to design a resume and professional portfolio. How will you stand out from others applying for the same teaching position? What are the key components you'll need to address in order to have a successful employment application and job search?

SUGGESTED READING

Campbell, D., Melenyzer, B. J., Nettles, D. H., & Wyman, R. M. (2013). *How to develop a professional portfolio: A manual for teachers*. 6th ed. New York: Pearson.

Part III

INSTRUCTION

Instruction or Instructional Delivery encompasses the teacher candidates' or new teachers' content knowledge and skills in not only the ability to impart information thoroughly but also in creating consistent student engagement and employing a wide variety of pedagogical strategies.

Chapter Seven

A Horse to Water

Shane Conrad

In this chapter Shane highlights challenges faced by teachers working in under-funded school systems, systems that can work against teachers by eroding their idealism about their work and by putting up barriers to the implementation of best practice.

I teach eighth grade English in Prince George's County, Maryland. Seventy percent of my students qualify for state supplemented lunch programs. Many come from broken homes and bring a broken view of education to a fairly broken school system.

My county stripped most of the funding for almost every non-Title I school. My building missed the mark of being a Title I school only by a little. (There does indeed seem to be such a thing as not poor enough.) This means I have zero classroom resources. I don't have paper. Imagine all the lessons you have designed in your methods classes. Now try to teach these without paper.

The year I was hired, not one but two English teaching positions were removed. I was brought in to take the place of two teachers. I have over 160 students, four classes of forty hormonal, unstable thirteen-year-olds. I have seen record high incomplete work, truancy, suspensions, and failing grades.

So far, teaching has been everything and nothing like what I expected.

MONDAY

I began the day running off copies. To the reader shouting, "But you said you had no paper!" allow me to clarify. I have no *provided* paper, but I am free to shell out fifty-five dollars a box at Staples.

The night before I had spent hours searching for a media clip to pair with Langston Hughes' "Dream Deferred." I settled on a news clip dealing with events in Ferguson, Missouri, and an excerpt from Dr. Martin Luther King Jr.'s "I Have a Dream" speech. I planned a discussion about Martin Luther King's dream and how the events in Ferguson reflect the slow march of progress envisioned by King, leading to the realization that still today racial tension is high.

To further contextualize the topic, I would culminate the lesson with a short examination of the poem "Dream Deferred" and have students write about their own dreams that have been put on hold due to life's unpredictable tides. I added a warm-up activity of independent reading dovetailing into peer edits of vocabulary homework and my 72-minute block was brimming with rigorous educational value. What could possibly go wrong?

Take a moment to recall how popular silent reading was when you were a student. Then consider that in an effort to increase student readership, I permitted students to use their cell phones to access e-books. As a result, I policed about 40 students with smart phones, only about eight of whom were really reading. The rest were playing games, texting, checking Instagram, and live tweeting, and in general sneakily not reading.

What to do?

Those who abused the cell phones lost them. Those who stared blankly at a page can stare at a zero for their work.

So silent reading is over; students are (not) working diligently on their readers' logs answering questions like "What surprised you today?" or "What did you learn?" or "What questions do you have now?" in four short sentences.

This is another blow you will suffer. You will tamp down your expectations to the bare minimum just to get students to complete the work. Daily reading logs began as seven minutes of writing during which students summarized the plot, answered one of those simple questions, and drew an image that represented something they had read. Several weeks later, the writing became four sentences that answer one question. Depressing, right? That is not the blow I was describing. The blow comes when you check those logs and find an overwhelming percent of students *still* not completing it.

We move into the lesson and the students watch a six-minute news clip outlining new developments in the Ferguson incident. As I prowl about the classroom not so gently tapping on desks to keep students' heads up, I am distraught by the lack of interest in what is one of the major news events of this year, perhaps decade. Just a few states away, fellow human beings are rioting in the streets, fighting police, outraged at what they have labeled a hate crime against the African American race and a gross abuse of police power.

My students can barely be bothered to pay attention. They realize so little beyond their Twitterspheres and Instagram accounts. I can't declare I was more worldly at their age, but I can remember watching on TV with my parents the Twin Towers fall on September 11, 2001. I was their age then. I can't help but wonder how many of these students would even glance up from their phones if such a situation were to be repeated.

Students then watched an excerpt from Martin Luther King's "I Have a Dream" speech, and I looked for some sign of emotion to flicker in their eyes as he hit those powerful words: "I have a dream that my four little children will one day live in a nation where they will not be judged by the color of their skin, but by the content of their character. I have a dream!"

And while I saw greater interest than before, overall I found myself wanting more from them. I wanted to grab them and yell, "Your life is the result of centuries of civil and cultural struggle and battle. Your right to communicate your every thought and action via that cell phone is something men and women have fought and died for. Respect and listen!"

But of course I don't yell. They wouldn't listen; they won't care. I can't make them listen; I can't make them care.

The aphorism "You can lead a horse to water, you cannot make it drink" is one I mutter to myself several times a day. Horse to water . . . Horse to water . . . So I ride on. I ask for impact responses, what we call "gut reactions" to a text or video clip. I get a few from the small number of students I can always count on, their responses a veritable life preserver that keeps me afloat.

This is how many of my lessons and much of my day proceeds. High expectations fall to the ground in fragments, and I begin to feel personally responsible for the socioeconomic disparity in this country. I feel like another cog in the machine that ensures the separation of rich white children from poor minority children. My students already occupy the lowest two economic brackets in the country. They have no idea how unlikely it will be for them to climb any higher without my help.

How can I call myself a teacher when there are students I have stopped trying to reach in efforts to improve my odds with those who have yet to slip down that slope? How can I call myself a teacher when I am starting to doubt the very institution I have identified as my calling and vocation in life?

But then I think of Tyra. And Erin. And Marques. And Aminah. And Adelabu. And many more students I *know* I've helped. Dozens of several hundred, but it's a start. I will keep leading the horse to water and ride out to the sunset with the ones who drink their fill.

While Shane's narrative is in Part III: Instruction section, what other domains are reflected in his narrative? What crucial conflict does Shane focus on? What teaching reality emerged as especially significant for you?

SHANE'S REFLECTION

After writing my story and thinking about it again with Danielson's Framework in mind, I realize reflection is an interesting process. I am constantly trying to find silver linings in my reflections as I review the day's successes and failures. I have found I have become better at Domain 2d: Managing Student Behavior to an extent. Managing student behavior means striking a delicate balance between keeping students on task and keeping them from simply distracting others.

I haven't found a way to get all of my students on board during and with all my instruction, but I have mastered keeping the ones whom I cannot engage from distracting those whom I can. That in itself is some days a miracle.

I have also found having strictly laid out and crystal clear expectations for learning (Domain 2b, Domain 3a) offers the best odds for student success. Leaving any room for interpretation only leads to students finding the quickest road to a complete assignment. If I outline exactly what I need to see and what that needs to look like, I find a majority of my students are more likely to complete the work to a satisfactory level.

I have changed many things as I have grown in my craft. My management strategies have tightened up, my expectations in certain areas have been tamped down to a reasonable level, but mostly I have scrapped what didn't work and elaborated on what did. I have routines in place that keep my students busy and keep me sane (Domain 3a). That's an important thing to find, your routines and your sanity. Trust me, you'll need both.

I have re-read my narrative many times since writing it last year. I have a new crop of students and a new year to experience. I unfortunately have found the problems are the same, the apathy is the same, the struggle is the same. I have found for my own sanity that having the knowledge my first year taught makes things much easier on my own life. I understand that there are things out of my control. I understand that I cannot change everything. I understand that my job is to be the best damn teacher I can be.

I will grow as a teacher. I will learn better ways to reach even the most unwilling of students.

SHANE'S INTERVIEW WITH JO-ANNE

During his post-reflection interview, Shane shared that he felt that his teacher preparation program had prepared him well for planning and preparation (Domain 1) and fulfilling professional responsibilities (Domain 4). But he made it clear that his successes were also contingent on effective management of student behavior (Domain 2d) and with his ability to establish a culture of learning (Domain 2b). He said, "So much is dependent upon this [Domain 2]."

For Shane, managing student behavior entailed efforts to understand his students' lives outside of school, a component of professionalism (Domain 4). He also remarked that what helped him during his second year of teaching was "having very clear expectations; for example, 'I want this many sentences or 'This is what I want you to do,'" these clear expectations a feature of a culture of learning (Domain 2b) and of instruction (Domain 3a).

Shane also put a finer point on instruction by noting the connection between classroom environment and instruction, asserting the importance of structure and pacing, two aspects of teaching a lesson that he calls "vital for effective teaching/learning." He commented on the importance of using a variety of modalities for learning, while stating that pacing, "while quick," still has to be responsive to learners' needs (Domain 3c and 3e).

To teacher candidates and new teachers, Shane states:

> You come out of your program feeling like a superhero, but you need to be able to be struck down. I have students right now who I can't teach, but somewhere down the road something that I said or did might kick in. Two months ago I ran into a former student who, although bright, barely passed. Now a student at a very good high school in Prince George's County, he said to me, "I wish I would have listened to you more." You have to believe that you're making a difference. You have to look at the bigger picture. I will have helped thousands of kids by the time I end my career. Reality and idealism have to coexist.

JO-ANNE'S COMMENTARY

After reading Shane's narrative, you were asked to consider what domains are reflected in his story. In his reflection, Shane refers to domains that he believes are integral to effective teaching, thereby demonstrating the complexities inherent within day-to-day teaching, as teachers are continuously enacting aspects of each domain, with enactment of domains and subdomains affecting enactment of others.

While Danielson's Framework for Teaching presents a template by which one can conceptualize and organize teaching, the reality of teaching is, quite simply, more complex. For example, Danielewicz (2001) characterizes teaching as a "complex and delicate act," asserting that teachers need to "constantly think ahead, to follow hunches" while describing the range of thinking that teachers must engage in as they teach, from analyzing the situation to considering their students to deciding on teaching strategies to implementing their plans (p. 9).

At the same time, the enactment of lessons that take into account the variables present in the typical classroom may be adversely affected by these same variables, especially student behavior. As Britzman (2003) points out, the "exigencies of classroom life" can undermine the teacher's relationship to "the canon" (the curriculum) (p. 73). What may result, then, is what MacNeal (1986) refers to as "defensive teaching"—teaching that results when teachers simplify knowledge and decrease demands to ensure some compliance with assignments (p. 191).

In his reflection, Shane writes that he "tamped down" expectations in certain areas to "reasonable levels." While it is not clear if Shane's decision to reduce expectations qualifies as "defensive teaching," the question of what can happen to real-world knowledge in a classroom fraught with a concern for student misbehavior and disengagement is certainly raised. Consider, for example, Shane's scaling back what he expects from students' responses to their reading.

"Emotional contradiction" is inherent in Shane's understanding of the need to balance idealism and reality (Britzman, 2003, p. 11). While, as Britzman asserts, "idealizing learning to teach is part of our dilemma" (p. 11), it may be that teachers must hold on to their idealism so that they can become the "best damn teacher" they can be to continue to lead their horses to water. For Britzman, "the capacity for contradiction, or the situation of multiple and conflicting meanings that constitute the heteroglossic in language, can serve as a departure for a dialogic understanding that theorizes how one understands the given realities of teaching" (p. 37).

FOR DISCUSSION

1. How does Shane's narrative show that teaching is a "complex and delicate act," as asserted by Danielewicz (2001)?
2. Is there anything in Shane's narrative, reflection, and/or final thoughts that challenges your beliefs about effective teaching? If so, what are they, and how might you reconcile this disconnect between your beliefs about effective teaching and the realities and beliefs that Shane shares?

FOR REFLECTION

In popular culture, the idea of "teacher" is often romanticized. You may have seen films about teachers and teaching in which teachers are portrayed as heroes who are able to turn disadvantaged, at-risk, and resistant students into high-achieving, compliant, and happy individuals. What reality (or realities) does Shane share that belies the notion of teacher as "hero"? How are films like these perhaps a disservice to the teaching profession?

FOR INQUIRY

In his narrative, Shane refers to his school as a "non-Title I" school; that is, it is not a Title I school. Engage in research in which you investigate Title I: What is its history? How is a school designated as "Title I"? Identify a few Title I schools in your county or district.

SUGGESTED READING

Kozol, J. (2012). *Savage inequalities: Children in America's schools.* New York: Broadway Books.

Kozol, J. (2005). *The shame of a nation: The restoration of apartheid schooling in America.* New York: Three Rivers.

Chapter Eight

A Tumultuous First Year

Richard Courtot

For "Ricky," working as a long-term substitute teacher, teaching outside of his area of certification, was daunting, however, this experience provided opportunity for a great deal of valuable learning about instruction and what it means to be a professional.

You are not always autonomous in your classroom.

I was serving as a long-term substitute teacher in a Title I school, filling in for a reading specialist and teaching grades six through eight. I was charged with teaching phonics to special education students, using a scripted program from a book purchased specifically for this purpose. I had *zero* faith in using a scripted program, but I had no choice. At the start of the job, midway through the second quarter of the year, I was directed to go back to the first lesson and re-teach all of the lessons that students had already completed.

In such a situation, what does a teacher with limited experience and working as a substitute teacher do? The way that I saw it, I had three options:

1. Rebel against the instructions of my supervisors and try to figure how to best teach these students on my own.
2. Follow the rules and do what I was told to the best of my ability.
3. Follow the required scripted program and supplement it with other (more effective) strategies and approaches.

Given my place in the school and my desire to prove that I had the potential to be an effective, full-time teacher, I decided on the third approach.

The first challenge was gaining the students' trust, because they had all given up on the class—and school, too. However, after what seemed like countless failures, they began to trust and respect me. Sadly, just when I felt that I was making progress and reaching my students, I received word that their teacher was returning, so my time with them ended.

As it turned out, the administration was so impressed with my work that I was offered two more long-term substitute teaching positions at the same school that carried me through the remainder of the school year, both of which provided me with the opportunity to continue building the relationships I had already begun to forge. One of these positions was teaching math and the other was facilitating a behavior intervention class.

I learned that a teacher does not have to compromise his or her beliefs about teaching when given a curriculum to teach or even a scripted program to follow. There are ways to adapt—to do what is expected yet to also tweak things to remain true to one's beliefs about effective teaching.

Before reading Ricky's reflection, consider the conflict that he identifies that can occur between a teacher's understanding of best practice and what he/she is directed to do. What aspects of professionalism does Ricky's story highlight and problematize?

RICKY'S REFLECTION

I will touch on Domains 1 through 3 of the framework to shed some light on how my teaching style and philosophy were affected by the situation I found myself in. I will follow up with some self-reflection and possible changes that I could have made that might have improved the experience.

The first of Danielson's domains is Planning and Preparation. For my first teaching job, I was assigned a total of three different long-term substitute positions within the same school over the course of a semester. I covered a special education reading class, a general education math class, and a behavioral intervention class. Two of the positions took most of the planning and preparation out of my control (because of scripted programs), but the behavioral intervention placement allowed me the freedom to focus on improving my knowledge of my students.

When your job is to help students cool off and get back to their classrooms, your ability to talk to and understand them gets a lot of practice. It was not uncommon for me to see fifteen to thirty students throughout the day, and my responsibility was to make sure that they missed as little class as possible *and* understood why they needed to calm down before rejoining their classmates. This experience helped me understand how to manage students' behavior (Component 2d) because I had to plan how to help students realize their mistakes and show empathy for their teachers and classmates before going back to their classes.

Each teaching experience also provided me with a different environment to test and adjust my pedagogy in real time (Domain 2). The "mainstream" general education classroom provided the most standard experience. In this setting, I worked to make sure that anywhere between 20 and 30 students were doing their work and meeting my expectations, both academically and socially. The behavioral intervention classroom provided the most intimate setting in which I was regularly helping students, either individually or in very small groups, reflect on the actions that had led them to this setting.

In between these two extremes was the most difficult test. Because of all of the instability in the special education reading class, managing classroom procedures and student behavior was especially difficult. It was in this place-ment that I found how effective compromising could be.

In all these environments, it was essential that I was flexible and respon-sive to students' needs. I knew that adjusting the lessons I was provided and responding to what my students needed were absolutely essential. Although I was against restarting the scripted curriculum in the reading class, that was what I was asked to do. But we worked through those lessons as a review to ensure that the students were receptive to revisiting the lessons. The reviews were not as scripted as the original lessons but aimed to assess how well the students knew the information.

The most alarming aspect of my narrative for me is my frustration with a situation that was out of my hands. Although every prospective teacher has a perfect classroom and course load in his or her head, reality very rarely matches that ideal. Perhaps many of the challenges I faced were exacerbated because students sensed my feeling of disempowerment.

Given the same situation, I think that I would seek out guidance and advice from my colleagues to help me feel comfortable with what was expected of me. This would have allowed me to vent frustrations in a positive way, while also helping me serve my students more effectively. Yes, the administration at the school saw my potential and provided opportunities to help me advance my development as a practitioner, but I could have done so much more for my students by seeking help and making better use of my resources.

RICKY'S INTERVIEW WITH JO-ANNE

In a phone conversation, Ricky repeated that the uniqueness of his first teach-ing position (serving as a long-term substitute teacher and teaching subjects for which he had little or no preparation) presented daunting challenges. First, because he is not a reading specialist, nor is he certified in special education, teaching phonics, even using a scripted program, was difficult. And he was also assigned a math class to teach.

Ricky made the point, though, that even though he didn't have the requisite pedagogical content knowledge to teach phonics and math, he positioned himself "to be successful." He worked to be able to fulfill his responsibilities, as he made the point that "teachers are always learning." He noted that he had to "adapt and learn how to do something," and that "having already learned to teach content prepared me to teach unfamiliar content." For example, he was able to use some learning activities that he had learned in his English education course of study. For Ricky, then, Domain 1: Planning and Preparation, took on a different meaning, as the planning and preparation included acquiring new content knowledge.

Another challenge that Ricky faced was using a scripted program to teach phonics. Ricky was uncomfortable using a scripted program, however, he didn't feel empowered to voice any objections to this approach. He also commented that he had been told to "stick to the script" but at the same time to "put his own stamp on it [instruction]" so he found himself "in the middle of differing directives." For Ricky, Domain 4: Professional Responsibilities, was "neglected" because he felt he wasn't "involved" as a substitute teacher. He did not feel part of the professional community (Component 4d). But now he realizes the importance of advocating for students—of being more understanding of and attentive to students' needs (Component 4f).

Although discomfiting, this experience piqued Ricky's interest in finding out more about scripted programs and curricula. He shared his interest in finding out the origins of scripted curricula and programs. Why do schools buy into these? What students do these programs purport to serve? Are there data to support their efficacy? Ricky went on to note that his school seemed to be using scripted programs for the "most vulnerable students." This wondering led Ricky to the larger question of who chooses and designs curricula, and he asked, "Why aren't teachers involved in this process?"

Ricky continued to talk about what he called his "tumultuous" experience while serving as a long-term substitute teacher. He stated that it "took a long time to develop a relationship and rapport with students." In particular, he voiced concern about his special education students, students who, he believed, had "given up" and were "uninterested" in learning. Because they had given up and were not interested in learning, they thwarted his attention to Domain 2: Classroom Environment: "Students have the power to work against teachers' attempts to establish a good classroom environment."

Ricky's thinking turned to issues related to classroom management. Having worked in the behavior intervention program, he had firsthand experience on a day-to-day basis working with students whose misbehavior was serious enough to have them removed from the classroom. He questioned the effectiveness of this program for dealing with misbehavior, wondering if it might be possible to help students learn how to avoid behavior that would get them into trouble.

With regard to student behavior, could schools be preemptive rather than reactive? Perhaps conflict resolution and/or problem-solving courses could be implemented. Could classes include discussions of appropriate and inappropriate behaviors to help alleviate problems? Ricky also wondered about the value of "using language for reflection" because he had used questions to prompt students to articulate their feelings, hoping to lead them to an understanding of their misbehavior and its effects on teachers.

JO-ANNE'S COMMENTARY

Ricky's narrative, reflection, and concluding thoughts demonstrate the role of Domain 4: Professional Responsibilities, in a teacher's life (even a substitute teacher's life). Because as a substitute teacher Ricky did not feel part of a professional community (Component 4d), he did not feel as if he could voice any objections to using a scripted program.

Included with Participating in a Professional Community is "relationship with colleagues," and included with Growing and Developing Professionally is "receptivity to feedback from colleagues." In retrospect, Ricky better understands how important this relationship can be, as colleagues can provide direction and support, while also indicating that he would not only seek out colleagues for advice but would also be amenable to their feedback.

Ricky's reflection also demonstrates his growth as a professional (Component 4f), given that his concern was for "service to students." He worried that despite his efforts to hide his frustration that his students were adversely affected. Ultimately, Ricky wanted to ensure that his students were being served to the best of his ability, certainly one of his professional responsibilities (Domain 4).

Clearly, Domain 4 is an integral component of teaching, yet, as Ricky's narrative, reflection, and final thoughts indicate, teachers, especially new teachers, must make a conscious effort to enact professional responsibilities. Although Ricky was a substitute teacher, he still had a professional responsibility—to serve his students. He believed that implementing a scripted phonics program to special education students was doing them a disservice, thus he should have consulted colleagues to ask for guidance and even approached administration to discuss his concerns, something he realized in retrospect.

Related to Domain 3: Instruction, Ricky's reluctance to voice his concerns about using a scripted program with his special education students suggests that he was grappling with the notion of authority. Authority allows teachers to function, to "carry out [their] role to educate students effectively" (Danielwicz, 2001, p. 170). Teachers earn their authority by successfully completing their programs of study; their authority is also awarded (through certification) and earned (through experience and professional development). Simply put, authority is power, thus teachers possess (or should possess) the ability to persuade students (and others) to act in particular ways. They also enact their authority by offering expert opinions.

Ricky was reluctant to share his thinking about using a scripted program; he was hesitant to speak aloud his concerns—to give voice to them. Yet, as a teacher certified to teach secondary English language arts, he certainly had expertise to share an expert opinion about sound instruction.

To better understand Ricky's dilemma and the reason for his reticence, it is helpful to consider what Danielwicz (2001) asserts about authority: "authority entails having a voice, the ability to speak, the safety to speak comfortably, the comfort of being listened to, and the power of being heard (p. 171). While Ricky possessed a voice and the ability to speak, he did not feel safe to speak comfortably, nor did he feel as though he had the power to be heard.

Thus, Ricky did not feel as though he possessed authority, even though, of course, he did, given his understanding of teaching reading and best practice. Of course, the context (substitute teaching) worked against Ricky manifesting his authority. Yet, as Ricky notes, discussing his worries with colleagues would have allowed him to safely exercise his power. Because voice is multiple and dependent upon context, practice with voicing his opinion and sharing his expert opinion with colleagues perhaps would have encouraged him to share his opinion with administration.

Finally, Ricky's first teaching job foregrounds a tension often inherent in the profession—that of the conflicting agendas of stakeholders. Different groups have stakes in public education, and these different groups want different things from schools. Businesses want schools to produce workers with sufficient education to successfully complete the work required of them. Policy makers may be concerned with producing future leaders. Parents may see education as a means of gaining social status and economic independence. Students, too, may have expectations for school and what their education is preparing them for. And teachers are charged with attending to these differing, sometimes competing, agendas.

The thinking that was the impetus for using scripted programs for a particular population of students may have been the result of high-stakes standardized tests that purport to demonstrate student learning and achievement. Standardized tests of reading often include "reading on demand" and word recognition exercises. Although testing accommodations may be made, all students are expected to take these tests; thus, a scripted program emphasizing phonics for special education students might make sense.

Also, the use of scripted programs would permit any teacher, not necessarily a reading specialist, to teach this class, as he/she would merely be following a script rather than actually teaching. In this case, stakeholders may have been administration and the community, those interested in testing results, results that are made public and used to judge the "effectiveness" of schools.

Ricky found himself caught between his position as a stakeholder concerned with meeting the needs of his struggling readers and other stakeholders who were perhaps more concerned with standardized test results or even with maintaining the status quo by providing a specific type of learner with an inferior learning opportunity.

FOR DISCUSSION

1. What challenges do substitute teachers (both short term and long term) face? What are some proactive strategies that you might use as a substitute teacher to help you meet these challenges?
2. As a novice teacher, how might you communicate with your administration if you are asked to teach in a way that conflicts with your understanding of best practice? In other words, how might you exercise your authority?

FOR REFLECTION

Ricky's narrative raises several issues, one of which is ability tracking. What are your understandings of and experiences with this practice? Do you perceive any advantages to ability tracking? Disadvantages? Explain.

FOR INQUIRY

Conduct research regarding substitute teaching at a few different school districts. What is the procedure for applying to work as a substitute teacher? What qualifications are needed? What orientation is provided for substitutes? What is the daily pay rate for substitute teaching? What is the difference between short-term and long-term assignments? Do substitute teachers receive health benefits?

SUGGESTED READING

Burden, P. (2010). *Classroom management: Creating a successful K–12 learning community.* 4th ed. Hoboken, NJ: John Wiley & Sons.

Kozol, J. (2006). *The shame of a nation: The restoration of apartheid schooling in America.* New York: Three Rivers Press.

The substitute teaching survival guide. (2009–2017). Retrieved from http://www.teachhub.com/substitute-teachers-survival-guide.

Chapter Nine

Teaching to an Empty Desk

Edward Litzinger

Edward's narrative focuses on student absenteeism and its consequences including disruption of instructional time for teachers and students, unanticipated paperwork, dilemmas regarding student assessments for faculty, and the improbability of learning for those students.

"He is facing his fourth suspension in five weeks; he will have been absent more days from class than being present," a fellow teacher grumbles. The month is October. Mrs. Davidson shuffles through another packet of papers concerning the student's recently observed behaviors that she did not expect to be completing at 7:30 on a Monday morning.

The papers request information about the student's outward appearance, irregular habits, incidents of insubordination, number of times to be redirected, number of times off-task, level of participation, and a number of other items and checklists (all for a child she had been given zero opportunities to meet). Almost lamenting the probability of the principal resorting to expulsion, she utters the number of ways in which a single student can create so much extra work for teachers.

When "behavioral" students disturb instructional time, they must be disciplined if they are to be deterred from repeating the same actions. A teacher extends the disruption further to carry out the appropriate disciplinary reaction, and even further still, when marking notes on the necessary documentation forms. How much time, then, is wasted in one class period?

The student is either prescribed a referral, a detention, in-school suspension or out-of-school suspension. For two or three of these, teachers must prepare the assignments "to-go" like an express pick-up line; this takes an enormous amount of time which could have been used for carefully preparing more enriching lesson activities. The regular, cooperative students lose out again.

77

If the student fails to collect and the teacher fails to deliver, then the student only plummets deeper into a discouraging pit of unfinished assignments.

Student absences are predictable, even manageable, but chronic absenteeism becomes a colossal headache. Teaching an empty desk is impossible. Unless their parents are teachers and/or can afford the time to instruct at home (which is mostly not the case), absent students are not learning. Those students can continue approaching their teachers before, after, and during class time for missed work, but they are simply receiving tools without knowing how to use them. Above all else, how can those students' progress be assessed? Can evaluation adequately take place with only a collection of grades for take-home work?

Chronic absenteeism is an issue that should be resolved between the parents and administrators, yet it is often only left up to the teachers to work with it. What is fair for the student to achieve well and earn good grades? How is it possible to work in extenuating conditions? These are difficult situations that call for individual attention on a student-by-student basis.

Student helpers can assist in being assigned the responsibility of distributing materials to absent students and catching them up with lessons. Systems of "While You Were Out" centers could be established, for example. Most of all, teachers can communicate the importance of attendance and attempt to make the classroom environment one in which students feel comfortable, a safe haven where students want to be for learning. And as teachers, let us attend to our own attendance; we must be present to do our job, as our own attendance is, of course, just as tantamount.

Before reading Edward's reflection, consider the following questions:

1. Do you think student absenteeism is a problem in today's schools? If so, do you think it hurts the student more or the teacher or both equally? If not, what evidence supports your claim? Who specifically do you think should be responsible for students who are chronically absent and why?
2. Edward suggests some possible solutions to the problem of absenteeism in his last paragraph above. What do you think of his suggestions, and can you think of others?

EDWARD'S REFLECTION

After thinking about my story again with Danielson's Framework in mind, I realize that good educators should not allow themselves to feel frustrated with problems deemed outside of their responsibilities or control, especially when the struggle revolves around a student with a world of possibility ahead. There is never an absence of hope in a child. And why else does a teacher do the job but for the youth of tomorrow?

The progress of a group of students can sometimes be stifled by the actions (or inaction) of a single student, for example, in the case of group work where each student has a specific responsibility toward the end goal. The student who is present and disrupts class is comparable to the absent student who also disrupts class by not completing his or her part of the project.

I have worked with teachers who complain about taking on extra responsibilities for students who are actively disruptive during class but would rather have them removed from the traditional classroom setting. Some instances do call for student suspension, while others seem to be more of a gray area when attempting to make the decision. Part of the teacher's job is to provide attention to each individual, however, I understand how it might seem unfair if one child is taking time away from a whole group of cooperative students.

Teachers often seem more distressed about the paperwork and documentation that pile up on their desks for chronic absentees than the actual handling of the student by the parents and administration. But these tools are essential. Most of these documents are used by special needs teachers and school administrators to determine improvement plans for problematic situations. These are all responsibilities that should be expected of classroom teachers.

Danielson's first domain, Preparation and Planning, is of utmost importance as teachers should, after having gotten to know the students, cater to their interests, abilities, and learning styles. It is even better to become familiar with the chronically absent student and formulate lessons and activities in such a way that might raise the chances of the student wanting to come back and participate once again. Serving specific learning styles might involve incorporating the student's interests and providing approachable activities that can be easily understood and engaging for the student.

Nurturing the classroom environment goes hand in hand with planning and preparation. Most specifically, building rapport with students and encouraging them to build relationships with one another are the absolute best ways that ensure a fun and engaging community of learners. All students truly love attending class when they can feel most comfortable with their neighbors, as well as with the authority figure in the room.

I have found it best to consistently show genuine interest in the lives of students, without ever being intrusive, inappropriate, or unprofessional. Having brief, three-minute conversations at the beginnings or conclusions of class periods and showcasing interactions in the hallways with students or other teachers can make a world of difference in how the children will perceive the teacher and how positive relationships should be modeled.

Likewise, with demonstrating proper social interactions, Danielson's fourth domain highlights the professionalism we should uphold. If a student is repeatedly absent, a concerning note or call home to parents should reveal that their child is in the hands of someone who wants the best for their boy or girl.

I thought of how community involvement and extracurricular activities could definitely subvert the absenteeism of a student. Pry politely into the lives of questionable students, talk to them about where their interests lie, and ask them to participate in outside activities. I often have conversations regularly with students about the potential they may not have discovered in themselves or the loves and passions they may not have yet realized in their lives.

I share with my students how some of the best experiences of my life have been discovering the things I love most and the skills in which I excel (sometimes having to do with subjects I never knew existed). I enjoy trying to intrigue students with the vast body of infinite knowledge and facts in existence, that the world is exceedingly more beautiful and complex than math and English inside of school and their video games outside of school. I implore them to search for the subjects that interest them.

I have students with parents who don't ask them about their interests, who don't fret over their failing grades, and who are never found on the benches at their ball games. For those students, teachers could attend those games and make sure to let them know that their involvement is admired by the community and that their achievements are celebrated and will be remembered.

You cannot be an effective teacher without caring and conviction. A teacher's job is not to gripe about the work but to boost their students, so that they can one day learn to stand on their own and carry on that compassion for others which will ripple outward for all the world.

EDWARD'S INTERVIEW WITH LINDA

As we went through his reflection, Edward wanted to speak first about Danielson's component 1b: Demonstrating Knowledge of Students in the Planning and Preparation Domain. He explained that his experience so far has been that "reluctant learners have a complete disconnect from school." He went on to say that these students are "not supposed to like learning," and they are "never asked to think about their interests at home" in school.

Edward felt strongly that it was important for him as a teacher to keep up to date with what is popular in the news, with film and television stars, and music, showing his students not only that he was interested in what they liked but also that his interests could be vast, too, not just about English matters. He said, "Teachers shouldn't be seen as robots."

Edward went on to discuss component 1d: Demonstrating Knowledge of Resources and explained that good teachers should have a system in place that prevents taking too much of a teacher's time away from student learning and shifts responsibility to the students for their learning. He suggested that creating a space where students could help other students who were frequently absent and asking students who sometimes misbehave to help out with daily tasks took away some of the "authoritarian monster" image teachers may have and makes the classroom environment "less threatening."

Citing 2a: Creating an Environment of Respect and Rapport under Domain 2: The Classroom Environment as key, Edward believes that there has been a "visible impact" in his classes when problematic students have taken charge and have more responsibility to assist both their peers and themselves. He explained that active engagement in student interests, hobbies, sports, and media modeled both positive connections and treating students with respect; he stated that when teachers are very engaged with their students, it is reciprocated.

He added that this reciprocity of respect between teacher and student, once it is established, extends from student to student as well. Edward mentioned that when a respectful classroom environment is initiated, both teacher and students may begin to take more risks to insure successful learning. To this end, Edward created activities that his students enjoyed, like a classroom Jeopardy game, and allowing them to play music they selected in their headphones as a reward for positive behavior to build a good rapport and to show students he "cared for their well-being and happiness," allowing "not even one student to sink."

He also added that component 2d: Managing Student Behavior was something that he needed to be proactive about to avoid high absenteeism and behavior management issues; he said teachers "have to be 100 percent proactive rather than reactive in order to create a safe zone where students want to return every day, engaged and excited." Edward thought that this kind of classroom management "begins on Day 1."

He illustrated what he meant with a general example of what he called having a "flip-flop" personality, but not in a negative sense. He said when a student is disrespectful, a teacher has to address it, but a minute later, the teacher must return to being respectful of everyone again rather than continuing to have an angry attitude toward one or many of the students. Edward realized that teachers cannot dwell on students' past behaviors, and holding grudges would be "immature and not good modeling." He explained that he tries to cultivate a culture of "reciprocity" among himself and his students and between student and student, a culture where respect and the golden rule are reciprocated daily.

Shifting to Domain 4: Professionalism, Edward selected 4d: Participating in a Professional Community and 4f: Showing Professionalism as important components to ensure a productive learning environment for all. He detailed these two components by talking about how it was essential for him to continue his involvement with his students in after school programs within his school and by communicating with parents, two important ways he felt he could improve his students' daily attendance in school.

Edward felt that communication with students in activities outside his English classroom made for better connections between him and some of his most problematic, distressed students. He also recommended asking parents if their particular child could join any meetings he would have with them so that the student could share in the conversation and become part of the solution to any misbehavior; he would agree with the arrangement most comfortable for each family.

He recognized that the paperwork some of his peers complained about including keeping good records of students' behaviors, both positive and corrective, and records of parent conferences were as much a part of his ongoing professional development as thoughtful lesson planning and his own punctual and faithful attendance at school. Edward concluded that he still wrestled with questions like "How do you evaluate a chronic absentee?" He agreed that like many of the experienced teachers at his school, he did not appreciate students who were taking attention away from instructing the rest of the students in his class who came every day and who were well prepared.

But he also stated that although teachers want to do a perfect job and make a "lasting impact" on all their students, he realized that teachers "really can't be perfect" or "fret what is outside of your control." For the moment, Edward seemed satisfied with several strides he'd already made to create a welcoming place for everyone so that his students would want to come to school and succeed on a regular basis.

LINDA'S COMMENTARY

Students are not perfect; like teachers, like all humans, they get sick, get tired, get stressed, and need a rest now and then. Regular school attendance is generally characterized as missing five or fewer days per year, where chronic absenteeism is missing 10 percent or more of a school year. The reasons for absenteeism vary greatly. According to a forty-four-page study of our nation's schools by Balfanz and Byrnes (2012), "Students miss school for many reasons. These can, however, be divided into three broad categories:

1. Students who *cannot* attend school due to illness, family responsibilities, housing instability, the need to work or involvement with the juvenile justice system.
2. Students who *will not* attend school to avoid bullying, unsafe conditions, harassment and embarrassment.
3. Students who *do not* attend school because they, or their parents, do not see the value in being there, they have something else they would rather do, or nothing stops them from skipping school." (p. 4)

I recall when my younger daughter was in third grade, she kept complaining of stomach aches in the morning and did not want to go to school. At first I thought she was just having some "growing pains," as we used to call them, and that she would be fine once she had her breakfast and got on the bus, but I now realize that her illness was a very real category 2 above, stemming from a teacher who bullied the students and was frightening my daughter into not wanting to be there. That teacher impeded and halted my daughter's learning process and ability to function in school. I met with the principal and asked that my daughter be assigned to another third grade teacher. The teacher in question retired the next year.

I share this story because as a teacher educator and a parent, I know that sometimes student absenteeism has a very legitimate cause, and we as parents have to listen to our children and try to determine what is wrong when they want to stay away from school. Bullying, for example, is a very real catalyst for absenteeism for those who are bullied and can come from both students and teachers, staff, coaches, and parents.

Antibullying efforts have met with good success in many of today's schools, but even more can and should be done. Many students may want to attend school but simply will not because they do not feel safe. Edward is thinking like an expert when he explains that setting up a classroom environment where all students feel respected and welcomed can make the difference in regular and engaged attendance, which clearly was a direct impact on instruction.

Edward witnessed the kind of absenteeism that was brought about by the students' behavior while in school, behavior that warranted suspension and caused mounds of paperwork for teachers. New teachers must face the reality that record keeping and taking proper anecdotal notes are part of the teacher's job and professional responsibilities in helping all students to succeed. Teaching the whole child is not just teaching the subject matter content. Time has to be set aside for the additional paperwork in keeping track of each student's progress, both academic and behavioral.

Edward writes, "There is never an absence of hope in a child." His expert teacher thinking here demonstrates that he does not give up on any of his students and that he works proactively to create a positive classroom environment where students will want to come to his classroom. Balfanz and Byrnes (2012) explain that a "growing number of states are implementing or championing early warning systems that provide schools, teachers, and parents with on-going real time data on absenteeism and flag students for intervention and support who reach the 10% threshold or are on the path to missing a month or more of school" (p. 39).

Edward offers suggestions on how teachers can assist all students in having a higher desire to come to school, including taking an interest in each one's hobbies or extracurricular activities, having students assist other students, and communicating regularly with parents. Edward reminds us that teachers also have a duty to report to their workplace each day so that students see their commitment to the profession; and I would add that they should report on time and be totally prepared to instruct well.

These suggestions can and do minimize the additional paperwork of chronic absentees for all teachers, new and experienced. As Balfanz and Byrnes (2012) advocate,

Attending school on a regular basis matters. It matters the most for our most vulnerable students who live in or near poverty. Millions of students are currently missing far too much school, with multiple detrimental effects. Chronic absenteeism is a key driver of the nation's achievement, high school graduation, and college attainment gaps. The good news is if we do measure and monitor absenteeism there is quite a bit that can be done to improve it with existing resources. Thus, as a nation we must act, to ensure that our students are ready, willing and able to attend school every day. (p. 41)

FOR DISCUSSION

1. Talk with a peer, your cooperating teacher, or your university supervisor about a school situation that involved a student with high absenteeism. What adaptations did that teacher have to make for the student? What was the outcome of the student's success in that classroom? What plans might you suggest for that student to succeed in your class?
2. Consider the three categories of absenteeism listed above in Linda's response and discuss how you would talk with the parents of a student from each of these three categories about her/his absenteeism and what plan you might suggest for each intervention.

FOR REFLECTION

Edward wrote, "There is never an absence of hope in a child." What do you think he means by this? How does his statement impact you as a beginning teacher?

FOR INQUIRY

1. Research current statistics on absenteeism and what schools are doing in your own state's elementary, middle, and high schools to alleviate this problem and share your findings with the class. What trends emerged? What preventative measures are in place in the schools currently to counter chronic absenteeism?
2. Compare at least two different school district handbook policies for absenteeism. What do they have in common and how are they different? Which in your opinion is more effective and why?

SUGGESTED READING

Attendance works. 10 facts about school attendance. (2014). Retrieved from http://www.attendanceworks.org/facts-stats-school-attendance/.

Balfanz, R., & Byrnes, V. (2012). The importance of being in school: A report on absenteeism in the nation's public schools. Johns Hopkins University. School of Education. Retrieved from http://new.every1graduates.org/wp-content/uploads/2012/05/FINALChronicAbsenteeismReport_May16.pdf.

Chapter Ten

An Unexpected Teachable Moment

Michael Tosti

Michael's story celebrates a time early in his teaching career when he experienced a spontaneous teaching moment he had not anticipated when he planned his lesson.

I enjoy reading stories. Oftentimes plot devices and tropes are easily recognizable and neat. The use of foreshadowing hints toward something that will bring the story full circle. Everything is neat. Everything is anticipated. Everything is clean.

Teaching is not a "neat" profession. There is nothing monotonous or mundane about teaching. Every day will bring about a new challenge or scenario that requires flexibility and problem solving. We try to be as organized as possible, but we cannot stop students from missing class and falling behind. We cannot stop school pictures or assemblies. There is no prescribed time limit that every activity should take. That is why teachers must be flexible and bend to the will of the unexpected.

In the fall of 2015, I covered for a Business, Communications, Information, and Technology (BCIT) teacher who was out on medical leave. I was in close contact with the head of the BCIT department who wanted to make me as prepared as possible since I was a first-year teacher and a long-term substitute.

One day, I assigned what I thought would be a quick four question warm-up. The questions were projected on the board for students to copy. Next, my students watched a short five-minute YouTube video about cyberbullying, figuratively alluded to as the "virus." The video sparked rich discussion and I was forced to put my plans on the backburner.

A student responded, "If I stand up for someone being bullied, don't I then victimize and label the bully as . . . well . . . a bully?" The student next to her said, "Well, if someone is seriously bullying someone, then they deserve to be called out and made an example of."

How could I move on when two of my students were discussing the intricacies of victimization and labeling? I encouraged students to stand up for friends and not place the attention on the bully. I explained to my students that responding to a bully's taunts is not the same as being a passerby who lifts the victim up. When we react to a bully, they retain their power. When we place the focus on uplifting the victim, we take that power away.

With five minutes left in the class, I had already acted out three bullying scenarios with the help of student volunteers, and about every student in the class had shared. This teaching moment was a success, albeit unplanned. My unexpected moment was a pleasant one.

As teachers, we must try to stay as flexible as possible. Remaining too rigid or fixed limits our ability to troubleshoot in the event of an unexpected setback, restricting our ability to dive deeper into an unexpected teachable moment that follows the natural curiosity of the classroom. There is no set script. Every day, with a little anticipation and creativity, you will write your own story.

Before reading Michael's reflection, think about what you would have done in this situation and what you might have done differently. Consider the following questions:

1. Michael begins his lesson with asking students to copy four questions and watch a short video clip about cyberbullying. Why do you think this beginning led to a successful class period? What are some other ways you might have begun the same lesson?
2. What do you think about Michael foregoing his lesson plan, allowing students to take the class into an unplanned discussion? Would you do what he did? Why or why not?

MICHAEL'S REFLECTION

After writing my story and thinking about it again with Danielson's Framework in mind, I realize that instruction should occur naturally. I believe my narrative touches upon the third domain of Danielson's Framework, Instruction. Two of the subsections of the domain are 3c: Engaging Students in Learning and 3e: Demonstrating Flexibility and Responsiveness.

When I first began teaching, I would set specific time limits for each task in my lesson plan. Sometimes this is necessary in the fast-paced climate of education. There is so much for students to learn and only 180 days to teach it. Other times I cut short the efforts I just made to engage my students by limiting them. There were times that I would feel wonderful when I engaged my students, only to realize later that a stark transition between tasks created a disjunction between their engagement and the task at hand.

For instance, imagine if in my narrative I ignored my students' intricate insights about victimization and labeling. Imagine that I moved on with my lesson plan, only allowing five minutes for the introductory video that they urgently wanted to discuss. I had already bridged the gap between their interests and my lesson's agenda. I engaged their thinking, and if I would have moved on, I would have created a divide between the interest that they were showing in my warm-up activity and the main task I had for them that day.

I don't think that anyone can truly master teaching students who every year bring a slightly different culture, a slightly different form of generational thinking, and therefore a slightly different way of learning to the table. But one thing that I have learned that I can master due to Danielson's Framework is my own flexibility and willingness to respond to my student's natural willingness to learn.

MICHAEL'S INTERVIEW WITH LINDA

Michael focused on two of Danielson's Domains in our phone conversation: Domain 1: Planning and Preparation and Domain 2: The Classroom Environment, specifically Component 2d: Managing Student Behavior, and particularly the subsections of Expectations and Monitoring of Student Behavior. Michael explained that his original plan for the lesson after the video introduction was to have students create storyboards in pairs where they made up two comic-book type characters and completed six dialog boxes relating to a bullying theme following a rubric he designed and would later use for grading.

He chuckled, however, that he felt a "tangible energy in the room" after showing the video clip, and after reading students' body language and making eye contact, he made a "split-second decision" to let their discussion and the acting out of scenarios direct the rest of the lesson. He could save the storyboard assignment for another day.

Talking about how he understood the "interconnectedness of domains," Michael realized that preparing instruction and managing student behavior were often woven together; he felt this lesson was a great opportunity for him to build rapport and to "see things from their perspective." He took his cues from the students' reactions and said they provided "serious" and "valid" responses to the topic, not off-topic side conversations that he'd experienced in the past where students purposely "tried to distract him" and where he'd have to say, "Come on, guys" to refocus the class.

He appreciated "being in the moment" and recalled using "with-it-ness" he learned about in his methods class and from student teaching to trust that the students were learning, just a different way from what he had planned that day. He told me that "instruction was given, just different instruction" from what he imagined. He was "teaching *them*, not a course."

He went on to say that this lesson was a turning point for him in both gaining the students' respect and recognizing that some lessons weren't "arbitrary skills like letterhead instructions." He noted that after this lesson, students seemed more aware of bullying issues, as evidenced by one student in particular who came back at lunchtime a week later wanting to discuss the topic further with him.

When I asked Michael to think back and if he would teach the lesson differently now, he gave a definite "absolutely not" in response. He concluded by saying, "Teaching has to happen naturally." He felt that success with students, not necessarily specific to English education, but just in general, is to "let things happen authentically."

LINDA'S COMMENTARY

Teaching expertise grows, as Michael experienced first hand, while "being in the moment" with our students. Although Michael was clearly ready with a pairs writing activity that would have met his goals for the day, he trusted his students' genuine questions and was flexible with where they wanted to go with the discussion and creative dramatics. His planned storyboard could wait for another time.

Author Jim Burke writes frequently about how much questions matter in our curriculum: "Questions are the Swiss Army knife of an active, disciplined mind trying to understand texts or concepts and communicate that understanding to others" (2010, p. 3; see also Burke, 2006). Michael quickly recognized his students were raising critical thinking questions in response to the video they watched, and he encouraged their wrestling with the bullying issues they posed rather than moving on to satisfy his learning objectives for the day.

In fact, Michael did accomplish his learning goals for the day, just "differently" from what he'd imagined; and he gained more satisfaction and accomplishment in building a classroom community, allowing the lesson to flow "naturally," keeping it student-centered rather than teacher-driven. This lesson even had a residual effect, as evidenced by Michael's recalling the raising awareness of the student who wanted to discuss the bullying topic more outside of class a week later.

In this experience Michael was reminded of his prior knowledge to act like an experienced, "with-it" teacher. The term "with-it-ness" is originally credited to Kounin (1970) who described teachers consistently monitoring their classrooms for signs of student misbehavior, immediately responding to refocus students to be on task. After interviewing Michael, I would expand this definition to include that thinking like an expert also requires that "with-it" teachers are attuned to these teachable moments that Michael describes and captures, adapting his lesson plan for his students' maximum learning benefits.

According to Professor Marie Proto at the School of Education website at Quinnipiac University (2013), "Teachers are likely not born with 'withitness' but can make a conscious effort to embrace the practice. 'Withitness' sends a powerful message to students that the teacher is aware, cares, and that students will be held accountable for their achievement and behavior. Everyone benefits" (para. 5).

FOR DISCUSSION

1. What are some signs in classrooms you have observed or taught where students are genuinely asking questions they care about versus deliberately trying to go off-topic to use up class time? What suggestions do you have for off-topic moments in order to refocus students and keep intact a positive classroom community?
2. Michael chose to use class time in verbal discussion and acting out scenarios rather than going to his idea of asking students to draw and write storyboards that day. Is flexibility an important quality for a teacher? Is it more, less, or equally as important as meeting your daily goals and objectives? Explain.

FOR REFLECTION

Michael acknowledges in his reflection that the "fast-paced climate" of school often limits the amount of time teachers have for high engagement on a topic because of the sheer amount of material to be "covered" in the curriculum. Consider your own experiences with schooling and discuss times where you felt school time was either at a super fast or at a snail's pace. What factors contributed to your feeling this way, and what are some things you will do as an educator to promote consistently high engagement at a reasonable and appropriate pace while still meeting curriculum requirements?

FOR INQUIRY

1. Design a thoughtful unit or lesson plan where you incorporate one of your discipline's goal-driven issues with a YouTube video or film clip and prepare a set of open-ended discussion questions for students to respond to following the video.
2. Using Burke from the suggested readings below or another source suggested by your cooperating teacher or university supervisor, create an appropriate assignment with a grading rubric that you could use as the culminating assessment or evaluation for one of your teaching units or modules.

SUGGESTED READING

ASCD. (2016). *A handbook for classroom management that works. Module 16: Exhibiting "withitness."* Retrieved from http://www.ascd.org/publications/books/105012/chapters/Module-16@-Exhibiting-%E2%80%9CWithitness%E2%80%9D.aspx.

Burke, J., with Krajicek, J. (2006). *Jim Burke's letters to a new teacher: A month-by-month guide to the year ahead.* Portsmouth, NH: Heinemann.

Burke, J. (2010). *What's the big idea? Question-driven units to motivate reading, writing, and thinking.* Portsmouth, NH: Heinemann.

Proto, M. (2013). *Teacher "Withitness."* Retrieved from https://quschoolofeducation.wordpress.com/2013/10/07/teacher-withitness/.

Part IV

PROFESSIONAL RESPONSIBILITIES

Professionalism or professional responsibilities refers to the characteristics of the teacher candidate or new teacher that demonstrate ethical behavior and integrity in speech, dress, and manner, the ability to forge professional relationships both in the classroom and in the larger school community, and to continue one's own professional growth and development.

Chapter Eleven

Teacher-Parent

Tara Brodish

In this chapter, Tara shares her surprise at discovering one facet of her identity as a teacher, and she relates some of the "parenting" that she provides to some of her students.

After jumping up and down and updating my Facebook status to let friends know that I had been hired at a school that wasn't five states away from my friends and family, I wasn't thinking about becoming a 24-year-old "parent" to 150 children. The methods and classroom management textbooks that I read in college stated that I would be a "mentor" to my students. I guess the authors of these books didn't want to scare me by letting me know that I would be taking on one of the scariest (and most influential) roles of my life—that of "teacher-parent."

In my wildest dreams I didn't anticipate that students would seek my advice or ask me questions about issues that really matter in their lives. Yes, Picasso and Shakespeare are important and I was ready to answer questions about them, but when a student asks you the difference between a "viewing" and a "funeral" because he is soon to be attending a friend's viewing (and funeral) who just took his own life the day before, "teaching" gains a new perspective.

When I was in high school, I didn't ask questions like these to my teachers. Instead, I asked my parents or my friends. Many of my students, though, don't have parents, or at least ones that are involved in their lives, and my students' friends may not have parents either. I realized this unfortunate fact when some of my students revealed whom they live with. More than one-third lived with a relative, friend, boyfriend/girlfriend, their boyfriend's/girlfriend's family, or they couch surf, hopping from one house to another. Not only is there no one to sign their permission forms for field trips, but there is no one to parent them.

Daily, I teach my students how to wedge clay or smear pastels, but in between I also sign students up for the FAFSA (Free Application for Federal Student Aid), add money to their lunch accounts, describe giving birth, search for college scholarships, and my personal favorite, educate about using contraceptives. "Where does your father work?" "Why are you not eating lunch today?" "Yes, a lot does seem to 'come out' when you are having a baby." "Have you ever volunteered anywhere?" "You do realize that *that* is exactly how you create a baby, right?"

That I have become a parent figure to some of my students has changed my identity as a teacher. I do not have the option of brushing students' comments or questions aside. I worry about their futures, both short- and long-term. I choose to take on the role of a caring figure in my students' lives because I know that it is important and that they need someone to care for them and about them. Some of my students have no one to turn to for advice, and if I don't seek them out to try to help them, I am risking the chance that they will miss out on an opportunity or make poor choices because they didn't know better.

More important, my students know that I am helping them. They acknowledge that I am trustworthy and care for them, and that makes me feel as though I'm doing a good job. They know that what I say may be blunt, but that I am being honest. Some of my students may not know a lot about life, but they at least know they can come to me and I will help them.

My beliefs about teaching changed drastically when I started to take on these responsibilities. I don't blame the students or their parents but, rather, the situation. Traditional family units like the one I grew up in are very rare in the school that I teach in. Fewer than half of my students live with both parents under the same roof. If some students do live with their parents, it is often that they live with one parent or shuttle between both on a rotating schedule.

Before reading Tara's reflection, consider the demands placed upon her given the population of students with whom she is working. Do you see any of these demands articulated in any of Danielson's domains?

TARA'S REFLECTION

My experiences as a teacher-parent falls under Domain 2: The Classroom Environment, in particular, the subdomain "creating an environment of respect and rapport" and under Domain 4: Professional Responsibilities, specifically 4f: service to students.

I was twenty-two when I completed my student teaching and only 23 when I started to teach in my own classroom. I may have been at least four years older than my students, but I looked as young as they did. It took time for my students to earn my respect, and for me to earn theirs. Once they knew I cared for them, they trusted me and were willing to talk about their personal lives and problems with me.

While studying to be a teacher, I learned that I would have to establish a rapport with my students and earn their respect, but I didn't realize the impact that would have on my teaching style and classroom environment. Looking back on my narrative, I have realized that I have come a long way in the three short years I have been teaching. Things were not as easy as they are now. My students did not like me. They did not trust me. They even had a hard time remembering my name. They liked their old teacher and did not like the changes I was making.

It took a long time for them to realize that I cared for them and was interested not only in their learning but also in their lives. On Fridays I would ask them questions about their weekend plans and they would be reluctant to answer. But on Mondays when I asked them how their plans had worked out, they were surprised that I remembered and cared enough to inquire about their weekends. Slowly, but surely, I gained their trust. Questions about their weekend plans turned into questions about their hobbies and families and then their career plans and feelings about the future.

By the end of my first year, I had a few followers who didn't mind being in my presence. Somewhere in the conversations we had before class, in the hallways, and even during classroom discussions, my students saw me as a person and not just their teacher. In the following years it became easier to build rapport with my students.

I now know that establishing relationships with my students is important. A strong and positive student-teacher relationship can change how students view school and how they view themselves. I have also come to realize that I am not the only teacher who values and nurtures these relationships. One colleague bought a senior football player his letterman's jacket because his family couldn't afford one. A teacher friend from another district helped sign her student up for food stamps because the student wasn't living at home and was hungry. A principal purchased three mattresses for students after witnessing during a home visit that they were sleeping on sheets on the bare floor in the living room.

All good teachers value the relationships they have with their students. They understand that students need to feel cared for and that this may encourage the desire to do well in school.

As I evolve as a teacher, I continue to realize the importance of an environment of mutual respect in my classroom and the value of building relationships with students—relationships that sometimes entail parenting. These practices foster good communication between me and my students and between my students and their classmates. Because my students value what I say, they listen. The students whom I connect most with are learning more in my classes, making me a better educator. And, honestly, this environment of respect and caring makes the day much more enjoyable!

My students know they can ask me anything and know I will be honest with them if they are honest with me. Some questions or comments may catch me off guard, but I am truly grateful that they feel comfortable enough to ask me important questions.

TARA'S INTERVIEW WITH JO-ANNE

When asked to revisit her narrative and reflection, Tara exhibited a broader understanding of Domain 2: Classroom Environment, as she came to realize how management of this facet of teaching affects other facets. For instance, subsumed within Tara's perceptions of classroom environment is the notion of "service to students," an element listed under Component 4f: Showing Professionalism. The environment of respect and rapport that she strives to create includes both mutual respect and concern for students as individuals—individuals who may be struggling with challenges that put them at a disadvantage as learners.

For Tara, caring for students is "service to students." And this service occurs in an environment of respect and rapport. Rapport, Tara stated, means functioning as a kind of parent in some cases. Tara reiterated her surprise at what she called "academic parenting," wryly noting that this parenting ranges from helping students understand birth control to helping them prepare for college.

As she continued to discuss her teacher-parent role, Tara referred again to Domain 4, Component 4f: Showing Professionalism, asserting the importance of advocacy for students through collaboration with school personnel, such as the nurse, the guidance counselor, and administration. She also shared that in her district communication with families, a component of Professional Responsibilities, can be difficult, as parents or caregivers are often not available or are uninterested.

Tara's final thoughts also included discussion of the importance of integrity and ethical conduct, another element of professionalism. She stated that there is a "line that can't be crossed" when students are seeking advice and help and that teachers "have to be careful not to cross that line." She went on to say that during the first couple of years of teaching she had to "overcome" her fear about this. Now she understands the importance of consulting with the nurse or the guidance counselor or other school personnel when the issues and questions students share with her are beyond her capabilities or expertise.

Yet at the same time, given the effort that she makes to develop a good relationship with her students and the trust she has established with them, she realizes that in some cases students may feel more comfortable speaking to her rather than someone else with whom they are not as comfortable or do not trust the way that they trust her. With this in mind, she is also careful, then, not to dismiss students who come to her for assistance and advice while also realizing that in some cases, she needs to help them reach out to others in the school.

JO-ANNE'S COMMENTARY

Like Nicole and Edward, other novice teachers featured in this collection, Tara understands the importance of seeing students as individuals with lives outside of school—lives that may hinder the learning that should occur in school. For Tara, the notion of "rapport" took on a greater meaning as she came to realize that the concern that she manifested for her students led them to confide in her and to perceive her as a kind of parent.

Tara's story exemplifies quite effectively what Britzman (2003) asserts about learning to teach, that doing so "was doing something to who I was becoming" (p. 12). While Britzman is referring to her entrance into a teacher education program, certainly Tara, as a novice teacher, was continuing the process of learning how to teach, a process that included building relationships with students. She was becoming a teacher during her first few years of teaching, an endeavor that was also doing something to who she was becoming.

But it is only through hindsight that Tara began to understand who she was becoming and that one of the facets of her teaching identity was teacher-parent. As Britzman (2003) notes, the process of hindsight is a "deconstruction of experience . . . a work of thought, second thoughts . . . and, at its best, allows imagination its surprising depth and breadth (p. 13). Tara concludes that being a teacher means, among many other things, caring for students, working to build relationships with them, and, in some cases, functioning as a stand-in parent.

This understanding of teaching reflects Smith and Wilhelm's (2002) concept of a "social contract" that exists between teachers and students, a contract that includes the need for teachers to know their students personally and to care about them as individuals (p. 99). While the concept of a social contract emerged from Smith and Wilhelm's study of boys and literacy, it is reasonable to extend the concept of social contract to all students.

Although Tara began her teaching career believing that she would be a mentor to her students, she came to discover that some of her students needed her to be more than a mentor. Fortunately, she was able and willing to fulfill this expectation, however, we are reminded that students' expectations regarding the accessibility of their teachers can be challenging and even exhausting.

Like other professionals, such as health care providers and psychologists, teachers may experience "stress and compassion fatigue" (Yacapsin, 2011, p. 11). To counter this, a habit of self-care can be initiated. Simply put, self-care is taking steps to care for one's health—physical, mental, and emotional. Self-care can consist of a variety of strategies, from eating regularly and healthfully, to exercising, meditating, or keeping a journal.

Although teachers like Tara feel compelled to meet all their students' needs, even needs that are outside the realm of the academic, this sense of responsibility can take a toll. Thus, teachers, especially novice teachers, must be cognizant of the importance of taking care of themselves to ensure that their physical, emotion, and mental health is not undermined.

Tara's ways of thinking about this aspect of her teaching identity, functioning as a teacher-parent, moved from feeling uncertain and uncomfortable about helping students with sensitive issues to feeling more confident but also understanding that in some instances she would need assistance from school personnel, such as the nurse or the guidance counselor. In fact, as practitioner she was expected to act ethically and with integrity, thus she understood that there was a "line" that she couldn't cross. Another side of teaching thus emerged, that of fulfilling legal responsibilities.

Because she is a teacher, a school employee, Tara is a mandated reporter. According to the Pennsylvania Family Support Alliance, a mandated reporter is someone who is "required by law to report suspected child abuse."[AQ] Mandated reporters must submit a report when they suspect a child is being abused. Thus, if Tara suspects that a student confiding in her is a victim of child abuse, she is required by law to file a report. In Pennsylvania, where Tara teaches, reports are submitted to Childline and Abuse Registry, a service provided by the Pennsylvania Department of Human Services.

In addition to the responsibilities that Tara has as a mandated reporter, she must also adhere to the Pennsylvania Code of Professional Practice and Conduct for Educators. According to this code, educators in the Commonwealth "make a moral commitment to uphold" values articulated in this set of professional practices and conduct (Pennsylvania Professional Standards and Practices Commission 2017). Stated in Section 4, Practices, educators are expected to "abide by the Public School Code of 1949 . . . and other school laws of the Commonwealth." Furthermore, "[p]rofessional educators shall exert reasonable effort to protect the student from conditions, which interfere with learning or are harmful to the student's health and safety" (2017).

In light of this, Tara's "parenting" can be perceived, in some cases, as not only an ethical charge but a legal one as well. Violations of the code can result in suspension or revocation of one's teaching certificate.

Tara's story of being a "teacher-parent" is enlightening and indicative of the myriad facets of being a teacher. It also helps promote a deeper understanding of Danielson's domains, in particular professionalism and the notion of rapport with students.

FOR DISCUSSION

1. Tara shared some ways that she established a rapport with her students, including showing an interest in their lives outside of school. How might you establish rapport with your students in ways that are appropriate and effective?
2. What are some self-care strategies that you will employ to ensure that you will remain physically, mentally, and emotionally healthy?

FOR REFLECTION

The story that Tara relates demonstrates that good teaching entails building relationships with students. However, while these relationships should be friendly, teachers should not be friends with their students. What does this advice mean to you? How can a teacher be friendly but not a friend to his/her students—that is, not "cross the line"?

FOR INQUIRY

Investigate the concept of "mandated reporter." How did this concept evolve? Who, other than teachers, are mandated reporters? What kinds of training are available for mandated reporters?

SUGGESTED READING

Layton, L. (2015, May 12). Is the classroom a stressful place? *Washington Post*. Retrieved from https://www.washingtonpost.com/local/education/is-the-classroom-a-stressful-place-thousands-of-teachers-say-yes/2015/05/12/829f56d8-f81b-11e4-9030-b4732caefe81_story.html?utm_term=.097f72bbb3ef.

Safe Supportive Learning. (n.d.). Retrieved from https://safesupportivelearning.ed.gov/.

So what is self-care? (n.d.). Retrieved from https://www.uky.edu/StudentAffairs/VIPCenter/downloads/self%20care%20defined.pdf.

Yacapsin, M. (2011). Self-care for the student teacher: A promising new practice for teacher education programs. *Pennsylvania Teacher Educator, 10*, 11–19.

Chapter Twelve

Lessons That "Stick"

Nicole Frankenfield

*For Nicole, lessons that "stick" are those that result when teachers acknowl-
edge the humanness of their students, when they make efforts to connect with
their students as people as well as learners. Nicole's story demonstrates the
power that teachers have to teach lessons that transcend the classroom.*

Going into the profession, we wonder what lessons we will teach our students.
More important, we can't help but wonder about the impact we might make:
the shy student who finds her voice through writing, the stubborn boy who
discovers that reading actually isn't so bad. We are often overwhelmed by the
amount of "stuff" that falls under the category of the teaching of English, and
we do our best to determine which skills and practices are most important,
most meaningful, and most likely to be carried throughout our students' lives.

Of course, when I entered the profession, I knew that I would be teaching
much more than English language arts. I, like many of my peers, "want to
make a difference" in students' lives and view that as perhaps the most important goal to strive for in a teaching career.

However, in my early days of teaching, that bold intention "of making a
difference" was somewhat undermined in my weaker moments. I learned that
students were more frustrating than I could imagine, my positive attitude not
as strong, and the curriculum standards more pressing than I had anticipated.
In short, I sometimes got distracted by the business of teaching, of checking
off each standard, and agonizing when students weren't performing the way
I had planned. I unfortunately allowed these pressures (largely applied by
myself alone) to take out the "human" aspect of teaching I had once desired.
Sure, I still put forth my best effort to show my genuine care for students,
to create the impact, but it was usually reduced to a three-second greeting as

they entered my classroom, a few moments before diving into my ambitious lesson which I needed to shove into a 43 minute time slot.

I still struggle with this, but surviving my first year of teaching has offered some perspective. I remind myself more often to ask the questions that really matter, such as "What does this student truly need from me today?" If there happens to be a "teachable moment," what is the lesson that is sure to be the most valuable? The lesson that they will remember and use the rest of their lives? What is the lesson that will "stick"?

Sarah is standing in the sloppy line of students waiting outside my classroom. I greet them as they enter, trying to get in as many "Good afternoons!" and "Welcomes!" as I can. With this sixth period class, the much livelier and animated "after-lunch" group, I tend to get more pleasant responses than from the students in my morning classes. I see Sarah get closer to the door, and as always, I make an extra effort to form a connection with this shy, but kind, student who I've somehow had a heart for since the beginning of the year.

"Sarah! How are you today?"

And then something extraordinary happens. Sarah is all honesty.

"Not good," she says, the familiar shyness evident in her half-smile.

She tilts her head. "I just found out last night that my sister, who was pregnant, lost her baby."

My heart breaks as I see this beautiful girl, whose beauty cannot be hidden by that same hoodie she wears every day, begin to cry. Her blue eyes well up with tears.

I instantly pull her aside from prying eyes and I do something that's not listed on my objectives or a part of my SMART goals Specific Measurable Achievable Results-Oriented Time. I give her a hug.

I teach middle schoolers, who are slightly more huggable than high schoolers, but not by much. They've long since shed their "it's acceptable to hug my teacher" attitudes. But not in this instance.

"Wow! I am so sorry to hear that you and your family are going through this."

"It's okay." She tries to wipe her tears. "I know that some people think it's silly to get upset over losing . . . of getting upset over something like that."

"No, it is not silly at all," I firmly tell her. "You have every reason to be sad over this loss. To you, and to me, that was a life."

I give her another hug, tell her that I will pray for her and her family.

"What's your sister's name?" I ask.

"Victoria. Thank you."

I see a look of genuine appreciation on her face.

This exchange didn't even take a minute. It didn't even take place inside my classroom. The other students were unaware as they chatted among themselves not even pretending to begin their bell-ringers.

Some days, we teach our students about forming connections with the stories they read, how to determine an author's purpose, or to analyze character development throughout a novel. Some days, we actually manage to meet the standards, to achieve our SMART goals, to make sense of the endless data and apply our analyses of data to help us meet our students' needs.

And some days we teach them the hopeful power of a hug; of being prepared to listen when another person is truly honest about what she's going through; of letting them know that you will pray, support, or do whatever it is that falls within your belief system of "how to make things better."

We teach them that beyond the standards, beyond the objectives, beyond the grades, there is a person who genuinely cares and loves them, a person whose heart aches with theirs, a person who tries to be more than the three second greeter at the door.

These are the lessons that stick, these are the lessons that go beyond the clichéd hope of "making a difference." These are the lessons that truly need to be taught, the lessons that could change not only our students' lives but our own.

Before reading Nicole's reflection, take a moment to identify and consider the tension that Nicole's narrative exposes between the responsibilities of teaching and the need to build rapport with students.

NICOLE'S REFLECTION

After writing my story and thinking about it again with Danielson's Framework in mind, I realize that the actions described in my narrative aligned primarily with Domains 1 and 2. I initially thought that the experience related in my narrative was one that I could not have prepared for and did not necessarily "fit" into a domain. However, once I looked more closely, I realized that many of the components within the Framework are exactly what a teacher needs to possess in order to face the unexpected moments such as the one I detailed in my narrative.

Something that is even clearer to me now that wasn't at the time of my experience is that every student has a degree of baggage that may or may not impact her learning every day. Sometimes that baggage is minimal and able to be left at the door, and teachers can still expect engagement and subject-related learning to occur, but other days the baggage might be understandably too troublesome to be set aside without first being appropriately acknowledged.

Domain 1: Planning and Preparation, is reflected by the unexpected moment described in my narrative. I was prepared because I had taken the time throughout the school year to get to know this student. I had worked to build the teacher-student relationship to possess "knowledge of students' interests and cultural heritage," in addition to some knowledge of the student's "special needs." Although it may not be possible to have extensive knowledge of one student (let alone all students), I make it a priority to be prepared concerning this specific component, and I consider this a professional responsibility.

In my teaching experience so far, I've noticed that knowing even just a little about a student's family and his/her social and personal life can help to explain many mysteries or issues that have an effect on her academic life. An action as simple as my daily procedure of greeting students at the door is a way for me to gather knowledge and build rapport with my students. If not for this commitment to greet them every day, Sarah might not have felt comfortable enough to answer honestly my question of how she was that day.

Domain 2: The Classroom Environment, was also helpful to consider as I re-examined my narrative. I realized that the components that fall under this domain are what made it possible for the important moment in my narrative to actually happen. Creating a respectful classroom environment, maintaining classroom procedures, sharing expectations for student behavior, and even organizing physical space are all components that allow me to establish order and rapport with my students throughout the school year.

Though not specifically mentioned in the narrative, my expectations and procedures for the beginning of class are what allowed me the flexibility to comfort and focus on an individual student without fear of the rest of the class taking advantage of the situation. Because I spend the first two weeks of school going over and practicing with my students classroom procedures and expectations, the rest of the class knew that they were to complete their bell ringers or read independently while I was busy with another student. I also like to think that some of the students were behaving appropriately simply because they knew that we treat each other with respect in our classroom, especially when a fellow student is in need of uninterrupted, individual attention.

NICOLE'S INTERVIEW WITH JO-ANNE

In a phone conversation, Nicole re-examined Danielson's domains, including components and elements, and came to the realization that her brief conversation with Sarah during which she offered a few words of comfort exemplified an element of Component 4f: Showing Professionalism, that of "service to students" and "integrity and ethical conduct." She also stated that, in retrospect, the experience demonstrated the need to be flexible and responsive as a teacher (Component 3e).

Thus, while initially reflecting, Nicole saw her experience as indicative of Domains 1 and 2, she expanded her original interpretation of the event to encompass aspects of professionalism and even instruction. Furthermore, she suggested a deeper understanding of the importance of directions, routines, and procedures, as the procedures she had in place allowed her to take the time to speak with Sarah.

In addition to these realizations, Nicole shared that Sarah was always on her list to keep an eye on and that she worked to maintain a relationship with her throughout the school year. She remarked that "my favorite part of teaching is building relationships with students" and that she tried to "make all interactions positive." She also added another dimension to the importance of professionalism, noting that "it's really important to have like-minded colleagues" and that "weekly meetings help us talk about tricky students."

When prompted to share additional insights, Nicole stated that she loves lesson planning but that a great deal of time is taken with managing behavior. It's helpful, though, to have team members and team planning time. Nicole also honestly characterized her teaching goals, sharing that "on some days (okay, most days because I don't particularly enjoy analyzing data) my teaching isn't necessarily driven by my department's data goals, but by the students' . . . needs, whether they are academic, or, occasionally, emotional."

JO-ANNE'S COMMENTARY

Of special importance in Nicole's narrative is her belief that as a teacher she can "make a difference" in her students' lives, a fundamental way of thinking about teaching that she also ascribes to her peers and others who opt for a career in teaching. For Nicole, teaching is more than creating and delivering lessons; teaching is also about shaping relationships with students.

Nicole's teacher-self is committed to helping her students meet standards and objectives but also to meeting their needs as people who have "special needs" that are not only cognitive but also affective. She can only be aware of these needs if she has forged relationships with her students. Nicole's sense of self as a teacher is thus informed by her understanding of the learners under her care. In the case of Sarah, Nicole had to move to another facet of her teaching self, exemplifying an additional aspect of being a responsive teacher. This move was only possible because of the ways that Nicole conceptualizes and thinks about her identity as a teacher.

Another key part of Nicole's story that informs understandings of teachers' identities is that Nicole must enact this aspect of her teaching identity (caring for and building rapport with her students) in a school climate in which meeting SMART goals and learning objectives is emphasized.

Nicole's identity (how she perceives her teaching self) may be threatened by institutional demands. It takes time to build rapport with students, and as Nicole points out, this time can be consumed with checking off standards and SMART goals that have been met, something that takes the "humanness" out of teaching. There exists, then, a tension between Nicole's desire to meet all of her learners' needs (the humanness of teaching) and her responsibility to ensure that that her students perform adequately. However, she also points to the necessity of seeking out "like-minded colleagues," peers with whom troubled students can be discussed and the value of team meetings to allow additional opportunity to discuss students' "special needs."

Nicole's ways of thinking about teaching exemplified by her narrative also demonstrate what Fecho, Falter, and Hong (2016) call "engaged dialogical practice," practice that entails that participants "be present, be aware, be open, be critical, be flexible, and be engaged" (p. 10). Nicole demonstrated her ability to be present for Sarah and her ability to be aware, flexible, and engaged. Furthermore, dialogical practice necessitates having personal connections with students, connections that inform the academic work that teachers do with them. Finally, Fecho et al. characterize engaged dialogical practice as "contextual, personal, social, and fluid" (p. 11), all of which are also exemplified by Nicole's actions.

Nicole's teacher-self informs her ways of thinking about teaching as well as her actions. Also, though, her ways of thinking about teaching inform her understanding of herself as a teacher. Faced with something unexpected, Nicole was able to act quickly and effectively. However, her actions were only possible because she was thinking like a teacher and manifesting her teacher-self. It is significant that Nicole did not take even a moment to ponder how to deal with Sarah; instead, she "instantly" pulled her aside and hugged her.

FOR DISCUSSION

1. In her narrative, Nicole shares with readers an essential belief about teaching—that teachers can make a difference in students' lives. What does that phrase mean to you? What does it mean to make a difference in a student's life? Do you see this as a goal for yourself as a teacher?

2. The importance of having in place procedures and routines is demonstrated by Nicole's story. What are some procedures and routines that you will have in place in your own classroom to ensure that instructional time is used efficiently?

FOR REFLECTION

After Sarah shares with Nicole what she is upset about, Nicole pulls her aside and offers sympathy. She also hugs her. What is your thinking about this action? What issues or questions does it raise in your mind? Would you have hugged Sarah? Why/why not?

FOR INQUIRY

Nicole's school's concern for and focus on results and data are a result of the prescriptive nature of the No Child Left Behind (NCLB) act that was enacted in 2002. The new Every Student Succeeds Act (ESSA) was signed into law by President Obama in December 2015 and was designed, in part, to "fix" NCLB and, among other things, places less emphasis on standardized testing results. What are some other important components of ESSA that will have an effect on public schools and teachers? Is ESSA a better law than NCLB?

SUGGESTED READING

Fecho, B. (2011). *Teaching for the students: Habits of heart, mind, and practice in the engaged classroom*. New York: Teachers College Press.
Fecho, B., Falter, M., & Hong, X. (Eds.). (2016). *Teaching outside the box but inside the standards: Making room for dialogue*. New York: Teachers College Press.
Kessler, R. (2000). *The soul of education: Helping students find connections, compassion, and character in school*. Alexandria, VA: Association for Supervision and Curriculum Development.

Chapter Thirteen

Teaching a Student with Depression

Patrick Gahagan

Patrick's narrative addresses a student in his class who struggled with anxiety and depression and how he relied on a community of professionals to help him create a safe space for the student to achieve.

Upon arriving at the junior high school where I'd be student teaching, I felt extremely welcomed by the students, staff, and administrators. Administrators do their best to accommodate all students and teachers, while the teachers try to find the right services for the students so they can succeed. This process works for most students but can be trying for students who have issues that do not qualify them for the types of assistance that they may truly need.

Struggling to cope, Ali finds school to be a very overwhelming experience and needs to have a significant amount of assistance in order to make it through the day. This not only has become a problem for her and her family, but it also has me worried as a new educator. Surprisingly, Ali is one of a few students who has a complication that hinders her progress in school but does not qualify to receive an Individualized Education Plan (IEP). Unfortunately, Ali wrestles with mental illness, including severe depression and anxiety.

My cooperating teacher and I received this information via a meeting with Ali's mother during the second week of school. Her mother outlined all of her daughter's conditions and informed us that her daughter also has many thoughts of self-mutilation and has attempted suicide. Ali has never had an issue with bullying but still struggles with making it through a regular day. I have many worries about how I can educate Ali without making her feel out of place. I also wonder how far I should push her if she becomes resistant in completing an assignment or project.

Trying to walk the line of being an effective educator while using Ali's classroom time wisely and making her feel comfortable in my classroom is stressful to me as a student teacher. Understanding how to meet a student's needs that are fragile and require resources that can help her become a functioning member of our classroom/school community is an area of teaching that I have not had the greates amount of training in.

I have taken a class that deals with students who have special needs, but the class did not address any situations such as this. A student's mental health was not reviewed in a great depth. Upon completing this college course, I felt prepared and thought that I could deal with all types of learners in my classroom. However, the solution to this situation is much more complex than moving a student to the front of the room or providing an adapted reading for the student.

The solution to my problem was intricate and required the help of other staff members in my school. After I was given the history of Ali's mental health issues, I wanted to sit down with her and my cooperating teacher to talk about any problems that she may be having in our classroom. Also, I wanted her to know that she could always tell us if she was feeling overwhelmed in our class and that she should not internalize her anxiety.

After our sit-down conversation, I maintained an open line of communication through my cooperating teacher with Ali's mom, our school's guidance counselor, and the vice principal. Our lines of communication were very successful in addressing any issues that might arise with Ali and helped me feel comfortable with the workload and types of activities that Ali would have to complete in my classroom.

The complexity of this issue and the number of steps that I had to take in order to know that Ali was comfortable in my classroom makes me wonder what I could have done to be better prepared for a situation like this. I wonder how I could have minimized the learning curve that came with having a unique student like Ali in my classroom.

Moving forward, it would have been useful to have access to narratives like mine so that we could be adequately prepared for these issues. Being able to discuss, analyze, and deliberate these situations will help new teachers become more familiar with the methods they can implement in their classroom in order to benefit different types of students.

The discussion of hypothetical scenarios would help new teachers and professors create a dialogue about these non-standard issues that arise in the classroom. I think that if I asked more questions about these issues, I might have been better prepared for this situation. Some questions that I might have asked are: How do you guide and teach a student that is known for having thoughts of suicide or self-mutilation? What should a teacher do if a student is depressed but masks their depression while in school? How do you get a student to trust you enough to tell you when they are upset or are overwhelmed?

Regrettably, I did not know that I needed to ask these questions as a prospective student teacher. However, the discussion and record of this scenario should be addressed in future methods classrooms. Hopefully this will aid teachers who are presented with similar situations during their student teaching experiences or their first years as full-time educators.

Before reading Patrick's reflection, think about how you would have handled this situation and what you might have done differently. Consider and respond to the following questions:

1. Have you ever been in a classroom where a student has demonstrated anxiety or depression? If so, what are the visible and perhaps subtle signs, signals, or behaviors exhibited by the student? How did the teacher respond? How did you or other students respond?

2. What classes in your teacher preparation program are preparing you for students who have no IEP's but who nonetheless have incapacities that may prohibit them and others around them from learning? Do you feel like Patrick that your preparation program should do more in this area? What else can be done?

PATRICK'S REFLECTION

After reflecting on my narrative with Danielson's Framework in mind, I realize that I was meeting many of the components in Domain 2 and Domain 4. Through many hours of observation and eventual practice in the classroom, I noticed that these domains can be the most challenging to meet because they have many unknown variables that can influence a teacher's ability to meet these requirements.

More specifically, the students themselves and their families can be unknown variables that we must work with when trying to create a classroom community that is effective. Case in point, the teacher-to-student relationship that I tried to build with Ali was one that not only needed the cooperation of Ali, but the cooperation of her mother and the other staff members at the school.

I fulfilled many components of Domain 2 through conferences among Ali, myself, and my cooperating teacher. Also, I met aspects in Domain 2 through the creation of our classroom rules and the overall communication that I had with Ali. I tried to create a classroom environment that would let Ali be independent if she wanted to be while letting her know that she should feel free to open up to me if she felt anxious in my classroom. The network that was in place among myself, my cooperating teacher, Ali's mother, the guidance counselor, and the vice principal helped me meet many components in Domain 4.

All of the steps that I took to resolve the concerns between Ali and our school environment helped me realize many things about myself as a prospective teacher. The first aspect is that I care deeply about every student in my classroom. Looking back at my many years as a student, I can say that I have had some effective educators and some ineffective educators. The goal for my classroom is to facilitate my students' abilities to enjoy their time in the classroom and for them actually gain and retain the new knowledge that I hope to pass on to them. The easiest way for a teacher to make this happen is to actually care for his or her students.

Another aspect that I realized about myself is that I cannot resolve problems like Ali's alone. Considering the situation that Ali was in, it would be ineffective for me to "go rogue" and work independently from others who know more about Ali than I do. The creation of our network was effective in keeping Ali on track in my classroom and minimized the number of interruptions in her ability to learn. This personal revelation will help me in my future classroom and hopefully will benefit my students as well. I was able to meet many components of Danielson's Domains 2 and 4 while trying to help Ali integrate into our classroom community.

Also, I was able to discover and magnify aspects of myself that I did not initially notice. Helping my students focus on learning and enjoy the process of learning new information is my goal as an educator. It is rewarding for me to think that I might have accomplished that goal with Ali in mind.

PATRICK'S INTERVIEW WITH LINDA

When I asked Patrick to say more about any subcategories in the Domains 2 and 4 that stood out to him, he went right to Domain 2's subcategory 2e: Organizing Physical Space, addressing the issue of safety in the classroom and how important it was for Ali to have a "safe space" to be "free to express herself" and "make mistakes" without embarrassment. Patrick talked about the line between checking in with Ali so that she did not feel alone but also not being "hyper-attentive" and hovering over her too much. Patrick said that his main goal was to help Ali become more autonomous, letting go of "constant prodding" to make sure she was keeping up in class.

He later emphasized 2a) Creating an Environment of Respect and Rapport and 2b: Establishing a Culture for Learning, acknowledging the importance of equitable opportunities for all students and with specific reference to Ali, his concern was about the balance of giving her space yet knowing "how far to push her." His general message to me was how he could develop a better rapport with all of his students and maintain consistency in relating to the whole class while attending to students who needed more attention.

In response to Domain 4, Patrick identified 4d: Participating in a Professional Community and again mentioned the professional services and resources he had to draw on from his school site. Knowing that Ali did not have a person assigned to her for an IEP, he realized she would need a "web of people" to help her resolve the issues that surrounded her inability to do well in school.

In further conversation with Patrick, I learned that Ali's mother was resistant to a "special program" for Ali because she did not want to segregate her even more from her classmates. Through a joint meeting with Patrick, his cooperating teacher, Ali's mother, and the guidance counselor, Patrick shared that he cultivated a relationship with these colleagues who were "totally professional," who did not "gossip," and who "streamlined" stating the issues surrounding Ali's inabilities to complete assignments; negotiating and collaborating as a team, they were able to propose actions that began to resolve some of the issues Ali faced in Patrick's class.

Patrick explained that when he later sat down with Ali herself and his cooperating teacher to begin implementing a plan that would help Ali, she was at first resistant and stated that there were a lot of comments "about" her and not "to" her. Patrick noted "how smart she was" and related to me that Ali began to respond well after she recognized everyone was making an effort to help her succeed (e.g., she took homework home and completed it; she felt safe to share her feelings with the guidance counselor).

When I asked Patrick if any other Danielson Domains played a role in his narrative, Patrick noted Domain 3: Instruction and Component, 3d: Using Assessment in Instruction—Feedback to Students. When Ali completed a writing assignment in his class, Patrick said he was careful to comment on "more good than bad" to boost Ali's confidence, but he did not "shy away from the truth" and did not give her "special treatment"; he believed he gave Ali honest criticism and was "priming" her for future assignments.

Admittedly, Ali's progress through the fifteen weeks of Patrick's student teaching may have been slower than for other students in his class, but by the end of his field experience, he noted that Ali was less resistant to work she didn't want to do. Patrick exclaimed somewhat triumphantly, "Her work might have been late but she still turned it in, and she stood up and gave a presentation which she'd never do before."

LINDA'S COMMENTARY

Patrick's narrative reminds us that both our students and new teachers are vulnerable when students' mental states affect their abilities to function on a daily basis. Current statistics from the National Alliance on Mental Illness (NAMI, 2016) show that one in five children suffer from mental illnesses including ADHD, anxiety and bipolar, dissociative, obsessive-compulsive, eating, and post traumatic stress disorders, to name a few. According to NAMI, only 20 percent of these students actually get help, and about 5 percent of students 14 or older with mental health conditions will drop out of school (NAMI, 2016, para. 3). Students already suffering from mental health conditions including depression, anxiety, violent behaviors to themselves or others, and suicidal thoughts by age fourteen may take eight to ten more years for them to seek and receive treatment. And students annually experiencing at least "one major depressive episode" have increased about 3 percent from 8 to 11 percent on national average since 2011, according to *The Boston Globe* (Vaznis, 2016, para. 14).

Suicide is the second leading cause of death for those between ages 15 and 24, and according to Diana Hoguet (2016) in "How We Can Responsibly Talk to Children about Suicide," "For every suicide that occurs, there is usually at least one child impacted. For the roughly 40,000 suicides that occur annually, there are thousands of child survivors who live with the emotional consequences" (2016, para. 1).

NAMI suggests that teachers and students together should become aware of the following points about mental health issues and provides a fifty-minute video including:

- Early warning signs
- Facts and statistics about youth and mental health conditions
- When, where, and how to get help for themselves or their friends
- When it's not okay to keep a secret (NAMI, 2016, para. 4)

In our own state of Pennsylvania, efforts through teacher preparation organizations such as the Pennsylvania Association of Colleges and Teacher Educators (PAC-TE) pledge their commitment to keep our schools safe and to prepare teachers for a better understanding of all the students they teach. A subcommittee of PAC-TE, the School Safety and the Prevention of Violence

Committee, was founded in 2013 as a source of information and assistance to both new and experienced teachers who are looking for resources to help students feel they can achieve in school without threats to their physical and mental safety and security. Their mission statement reads:

> Committed to safe schools and by extension safe communities, the committee believes that pre-service teachers should be prepared to help ALL students to learn and feel safe and accepted in their schools and communities. Pre-service teachers should exhibit empathy and compassion for ALL students and try to holistically understand what children are experiencing. (PAC-TE, 2016)

To meet these goals, the PAC-TE subcommittee has developed a series of modules for all teacher preparation programs available on its website, www.pac-te.org, for better understanding of mental health concerns including bullying, grief and loss, and suicide prevention. NAMI and PAC-TE are just two of the countless organizations, books, articles, and websites that are assisting teachers and their students in coping with the pressures of school, home, peers, and other cultural and social factors that impact both mental and physical health.

While probably nothing better could take the place of the live experience of Patrick forming a professional community with his cooperating teacher, counselor, administration, and Ali's mother to aid Ali in succeeding, perhaps access to resources like these would have prepared Patrick more to understand students like Ali in his methods courses before student teaching.

And while more knowledge is always more power in enabling new teachers to function like experts, the most important take-away from Patrick's narrative is that he cared; he "cared deeply" about Ali's well-being from the very first days of school, and he cared about how he occupied the space with her in his classroom, how his tone and mannerisms—manifested in his written, verbal, and physical feedback—would affect her ability (and all of his students) to function and thrive in his classroom.

Patrick's narrative and the Danielson domains he reflected on reminds us that thinking like an expert requires forming professional communities with key players (Domain 4) so that we can assist our students on a one-on-one basis in our daily classrooms (Domains 2 and 3). And most important, caring about all of our students is thinking like an expert teacher.

FOR DISCUSSION

1. Patrick mentions that he created a set of classroom rules that he went over with Ali and her classmates at the beginning of the school year. What do

you think a set of classroom rules should include? What is your rationale
for creating these rules?
2. As Patrick suggests, discuss some real or imagined scenarios for student
    behaviors that would be disruptive to the learning of themselves and/or
    students around them. What contingency plans would you have in place
    for coping with student resistance or disruption?

FOR REFLECTION

Think about a teacher that really cared about you and one that you felt did not.
Make a list of qualities of a caring teacher and compare it to a list of one that
is not caring. Why is it important for teachers to care about their students?

FOR INQUIRY

1. Research your local mental health organizations and websites to find out
    where you can get more advice about helping others who have mental
    health conditions.
2. Choose a specific and focused mental health issue you are passionate
    about and prepare a PowerPoint or Prezi and talk you could give to your
    colleagues in a school in-service program that would assist them in help-
    ing students in their classes.

SUGGESTED READING

Burden, P. (2016). *Classroom management: Creating a successful K-12 learning
    community*. 6th ed. Indianapolis: John Wiley & Sons.
Carolla, Bob. (2016, September 28). MediaWatch: Reporting on Suicide. Retrieved
    from https://www.nami.org/Blogs/NAMI-Blog/September-2016/MediaWatch-
    Reporting-on-Suicide#sthash.W5HyJYet.dpuf.
Houguet. D. (2016, September 21). How we can responsibly talk to children about sui-
    cide. Retrieved from https://www.nami.org/Blogs/NAMI-Blog/September-2016/
    How-We-Can-Responsibly-Talk-to-Children-About-Suic#sthash.fd9dalHV.dpuf.
McCarthy, J., & Norris, L. (2013). Keeping candidates safe: School safety and pre-
    vention of violence for pre-service teacher education. Retrieved from https://www
    .pac-te.org/uploads/1443284139_PACTE%20School%20Safety%20Positon%20
    Paper%20Final%20Draft%20Oct%20%2024%2013.pdf.
NAMI: Ending the silence. (2016). Retrieved from http://www.nami.org/Find-Sup-
    port/NAMI-Programs/NAMI-Ending-the-Silence#sthash.YFLNJoyT.dpuf Rizvi,
    S. (2013). Mental illness in the classroom: How educators can help students suc-

ceed. Retrieved from https://www.studyinsured.com/health-tips/educators-agents/ student-mental-health/mental-illness-in-the-classroom-how-educators-can-help-students-succeed/.

Vaznis, J. (2016, May 16). Schools struggle to cope with rising mental health needs. *Boston Globe*. Retrieved from https://www.bostonglobe.com/metro/2016/05/16/ schools-confront-students-rising-mental-health-toll/J4nGkaSYW23qDbmQ2Pm-jLO/story.html.

Chapter Fourteen

The Pang of Terror

Janel Prinkey

Janel's story describes two separate incidents in her first year of teaching when she felt unprepared to act when students caught her by surprise; she also includes her reactions to a school shooting threat she received during her second year.

"Ms. Prinkey, I think she fainted!" These words still ring in my ears two years after a student of mine had a seizure in my classroom.

It was my first year of teaching; I felt confident that I could handle anything. I dressed in clothes that were pressed neatly the night before, grabbed my lunch from the refrigerator, and headed to work. I taught eleventh grade English that year and had a wide range of students.

That day started off as a normal day. I took attendance and started going over the bell-ringer activity when I heard the concerned exclamation, "Ms. Prinkey, I think she fainted!" I knew that Rachel was prone to seizures, mainly due to the fact that I was given a 504 plan detailing such. What I did not know, and was not informed about previously, was what to do if she ever had one. I had asked at one point and was brushed off. Goodness knows, I could have used some advice.

I rushed over to the student who was convulsing and cleared the desks from her path. I knew that she needed to be on the floor and that nothing should be around her. Was that something I learned from working at camp over the summer? From a television show? Who knows. A few students in my class were volunteer firefighters, and they were quick to get help.

I sent a student immediately to the office and pushed the red button that was supposed to alert the emergency team. What I found out that day was that the red button, the button that was supposed to be our lifeline in times just like this one, was broken.

121

Soon the emergency team arrived, and I was able to get my small class out of the situation. I led them to the conference room where I tried to establish some sense of normalcy. I tried to curb any discussion about the student. I also addressed how we needed to make sure that we kept such things private, knowing all too well how the rumor mill at any high school can churn.

Not two months afterward, my class was interrupted by one of my principals. "Excuse me, Ms. Prinkey, but I'll need to borrow Johnny here. You. Up. Now!" Before I could respond, the student sitting directly in front of me grinned widely and then went with the principal to the office.

I did not find out until after the fact that this student had shown up to my second period class intoxicated. I had not even noticed. I immediately felt sick. Was I supposed to know this, too? What was I supposed to do? He normally puts his head down at the beginning of class. Does that mean that he was always drunk?

I know now that school is fast-paced, and that teachers work together to ensure the safety of students. That just because I did not catch it did not mean that other veteran teachers did not know what to look for. It was a relief and a call to action. I would make sure that my classroom was a safe environment, one where students would feel like they could express ideas and never feel the pang of terror that I had felt twice this year.

It was in October of my second year of teaching that I felt that familiar pang once more. I was on a long weekend break, enjoying some time with friends when I heard my phone vibrate. The school had a RemindMe texting system set up for the teachers so that we could be "kept in the loop" about all of the upcoming events at the school.

I was expecting to read something about lesson plans, jeans on Friday, or even to bring money for the school's latest fund-raiser. Instead, I read in panic that there was a threat to "shoot up" the school on Twitter. A student who had attended the high school years previously posted pictures of our principal, saying she was the next target, and warned students not to come to school if they wanted to live.

I reacted in a way that I was required to as a teacher. My administration was asking me to come in on Monday, just like any other Monday. Except this Monday, I might not come home. My administration would not ask me to come to the school if it was not safe, but unfortunately, it did not feel safe as a new teacher. I decided to come to school that day in spite of this.

The school was quiet on that Monday in October. I had two or three students in each class, and I went through my day thinking that the worst could happen. Thankfully, my principal informed us that the culprit was in custody, and that the whole thing was a hoax. In the aftermath of Sandy Hook, however, no threat feels like a hoax.

As a third-year teacher looking back at these experiences, I am filled with a sense of regret. I wish that I had not done that, or thought this, or wish I could have done that better. The problem with that method of thinking is that it assumes that I (as a third-year teacher) know better than my first- and second-year selves. And I do! But this is only because I went through those experiences in my first and second years of teaching.

I know now how to address a seizure in the classroom. I know how to soothe students in the fear of a threat. I know how to recognize abnormal behavior in students and the correct avenues to take to report that behavior. We fledgling teachers need to realize that we are not perfect packaged teachers upon graduation. We are continually changing models who learn more about the profession with every year that we spend in it.

Before reading Janel's reflection, consider the following questions:

1. If a student had a seizure in your classroom, what is the first thing you would do and why? What are some of the signs you might notice if a student comes to your classroom intoxicated or high? Again, what is the first thing you would do?
2. If you were texted outside of school that the school received a shooting threat, what would you do? What if the threat came when you were already in school?

JANEL'S REFLECTION

After thinking about them again with Danielson's Framework in mind, I realize that my experiences fall under the vague, but all-important Component 4f: Showing Professionalism. No one could teach me how to respond in a crisis. No one could teach me what to do if a student is drunk. And most likely, no one can instruct me on the next unpredictable occurrence that I will face in my classroom.

The plain truth is this: whatever you do, do it as a professional. I did not panic when Rachel had a seizure in my classroom. I did not lose my demeanor as an authority figure, even though inside I was feeling the adrenaline that comes with not knowing what to do. That in itself is learning how to teach.

Reading and reflecting on my story has reminded me that teaching is a great responsibility. We owe it to the students, not to be perfect, but to do the best with what we have at the moment, and to be the adult in the classroom. The statement that got me through my first two years of teaching was, "Fake it until you make it." It is, admittedly, cheesy, but I think it still provides a sense of clarity. Want to be a great teacher? Act like one. Want to be a model adult citizen for your students? Show them what it looks like to be one. We matter to our students, and so we are obliged to be the best we can for them in that moment.

Looking back at my first two years of teaching has allowed me to appreciate how much I am learning in such a short period of time. I have grown into a professional who makes the best decisions she can for her students. I still make mistakes. I still think about how I have handled certain situations in the past and cringe. We will always wish we knew then what we know now. That motivation is what propels us forward and makes us want to be better for our students.

I would not change a thing that I have done in those first two years, and that is because I have learned from my mistakes. I know now about how serious it is to have an adolescent in your charge, and just how unpredictable life in school is for teachers and students alike.

JANEL'S INTERVIEW WITH LINDA

When I asked her to reflect on Danielson's Domains, Janel began with the seizure incident and focused on Domain 3: Instruction, specifically Component 3e: Demonstrating Flexibility and Responsiveness, as she explained that she knew she had to have a plan and provide structure in an unstructured situation so as not to panic the students or herself.

She described the incident as a "quick thing" as her adrenalin kicked in; she described that she felt "a bit frozen, scared." Janel used her knowledge of students in her classroom to assist her; she told me that this group of ten to eleven juniors in her class included her "welder" students and one who was a firefighter who had some emergency responder training. The students helped Janel to stay calm and focused. Because she had no phone or working alarm in her room, she sent a student to the office for help; she added that five to ten minutes felt like a long time when waiting for the emergency team to arrive.

She also referred to Domain 2: The Classroom Environment and said she should have established a classroom environment so that the students felt unified to look to her for help and allowed her to be the facilitator. Looking back, Janel said, I "did what I had to do," but stated that the whole incident was not as "smooth" as it might have been.

Upon reflection, she stated that she would be able to separate her emotions from procedures now that she is "not as intimidated" and would be less panicked and rushed now. Janel felt like she wasn't doing all she could have done; she felt a "sense of dread" over the incident. She said, "I never thought this would happen." She told me that she "learned to go to the IEP

[Individualized Education Plan] person," now has an emergency plan, and knows when to ask for help.

When I asked her about "the rumor mill" that she seemed concerned about in her narrative, she explained that part of setting up the right classroom environment includes upholding the dignity of every student. Regarding the student having the seizure, she said, "She was a person," and that no one in class pulled out a cell phone; no pictures were taken. Janel hoped her students understood that this was a private incident that warranted no further outside discussion or publicity.

Janel explained that at this time, she was only six years older than her students; thinking like an expert, she was trying to model what adults should do by not gossiping about the incident. She added that she didn't know if this helped set the expectation for students not inflating an emergency situation, but she hoped leading the class to a conference room and returning to the lesson for the day was the appropriate measure to take once the student was out of harm's way.

In the situation of the intoxicated student, Janel remembered how the student in question reacted obediently to the stern, dominant tone of the principal leading the student out of her classroom. She was worried, however, if she would regain her English class after the interruption. She told me that the administration trusted her to continue with the lesson since the incident "didn't affect her directly."

When I asked her how the principal found out about the student, she said that she was "not in the direct line on this," and often, teachers were only informed about students on a "need-to-know basis." Janel surmised that the student's homeroom teacher may have reported the intoxication and that the principal was able to intervene by Janel's second period class.

Janel felt she needed to trust the administration to take care of the student and to provide an alternative environment once he was removed from her classroom. Her verbal response was closely aligned with her written response regarding Domain 4: Professional Responsibilities, particularly, Component 4f: Showing Professionalism in integrity and ethical conduct, service to students, and compliance with school and district regulations.

Regarding the school shooting threat, Janel reflected that "the whole scenario was so unreal." Remembering that school attendance was minimal that day, Janel mentioned the importance of parental involvement. She related that teachers almost have to expect trust between them and the administration, but "parental trust has to be earned in a whole other way." The majority of parents in her school clearly felt that having their children miss one day of school was better than taking the risk of a school shooting.

Pointing again to Domain 4, Janel referred to the importance of Component 4c: Communicating with Families. She recalled that an entire high school meeting was called where everyone present was told the person responsible for the hoax had been apprehended. Shortly after the incident, specific training on armed intruders was provided for all teachers. Janel conveyed that all teachers tried to come up with crisis plans for their classrooms. This involved thinking about what they would do to protect their students in case of a shooter. Janel planned to barricade the door while students were going out the window of her ground-level classroom and then get out quickly through the window. Teachers were instructed to think of these things just in case something similar might happen.

Janel stated that now in her third year of teaching, when the question arises, "What do you do when you don't know what to do?" she responds, "Have confidence, even when you don't feel that way." She related that she feels more successful as of late because she is building authentic relationships with her students. She explained that students "don't care what you know until they know that you care."

Like many experienced teachers, Janel is highly aware of the importance to "show students you are a person, they are people, your job is to help them. Show you care and go from there." Janel told me that the readings she had done in our methods classes about building these genuine, caring relationships have still resonated with her; she believes, "It becomes more obvious as you work with kids." She concluded that you have to "trust in yourself" and "trust in the administration. It will be ok if you have done everything you can do."

LINDA'S COMMENTARY

Janel used knowledge she had about her students, as well as her trust in working with the administration, to guide her in acting responsibly in three very challenging and stressful school situations. In the first incident, Janel wrote that she was aware that the student was prone to seizures from receiving a 504 plan, had inquired what she should do if the student experienced one, and was "brushed off." Unlike more experienced teachers, often new teachers do not pursue matters further when they do not receive immediate information about specifically what to do for any number of reasons.

New teachers and teacher candidates may feel they do not want to be a burden to more experienced faculty or staff by asking so many questions; they may think it is up to them to learn what to do on their own; or they simply do not have the time or inclination to seek out other mentors who will explain precisely what to do. Likewise, administrators may not always take the time and care necessary to direct new teachers or teacher candidates to the proper materials, mentors, or personnel they need to navigate in their unfamiliar surroundings.

According to Dr. William Turk, chief of the Neurology Division at the Nemours Children's Clinic in Jacksonville, Florida, regarding students with epilepsy,

> If your daughter has a seizure in class and the teacher isn't informed about epilepsy, the teacher will automatically call an ambulance. Not only is the ambulance unnecessary, but the frenzied emergency process may frighten your child and the other kids in class even more than the seizure. When the teacher has been warned in advance, she won't be surprised. (WebMD, 2016, para. 6)

Often overburdened and overwhelmed by just the sheer amount of new material and new surroundings first-year teachers experience in their early days of having their own classroom and duties, they can easily set aside notices they receive about students with specific health issues or forget to check for malfunctioning equipment. Only after the seizure situation occurred did Janel realize that the emergency button in her room was not working properly and that she did not exactly know what to do next. She exercised good instincts when she remembered some previous training she'd had from summer camp to assist the epileptic student, to send other students for help, and to move the rest of the class to a secure area so that she could continue teaching.

"He normally puts his head down at the beginning class. Does that mean he was always drunk?" Janel's response regarding the intoxicated student is not an infrequent one raised by new teachers or student teachers. The Substance Abuse and Mental Health Services Administration (2015) reports that "Alcohol is the most widely misused substance among America's youth" (para.1). Their website provides tips and detailed information on underage drinking and preventative measures for this threat to adolescent development.

Teachers with more experience recognize signals like heads on desks, sleeping in class, or other inattentiveness as red flags that something is wrong and that they have several options by which they can reengage the student including subtle tapping on the desk, approaching quietly to see if the student is OK, or arranging to speak with the student at some point in or after class time. Again, some students can go unnoticed as Janel stated because they may be almost invisible in class. They are not disruptive; they are simply there filling the seats.

Because new and student teachers frequently do not feel they have the same authority or ownership of the classroom as their cooperating teachers or experienced peers, or because they may fear the repercussions or loss of class time in calling attention to the student, or even because they welcome the peace and quiet of teaching their lessons without distraction from the student, they may overlook or choose to ignore inattentive behaviors once or many times.

Janel states that this incident was a "call to action" for her to create a "safe environment." She learned to look for signals of student distress after this incident, realized that she could not be passive about a student's invisible behavior, and noted that "teachers work together to ensure the safety of students," acknowledging that compliance with the principal and administration was necessary in this case for the student's well-being.

According to the National Association of School Psychologists (2015), "Administrators can reinforce the importance of creating a caring school community in which adults and students respect and trust each other and all students feel connected, understand expectations, and receive the behavioral and mental health support they need" (para. 3). And in her classroom daily, Janel began showing all students that she cared about them and was there to help them; her comprehension of honoring the "personhood" of herself and each of her students was the expert move she chose to create a more successful, productive classroom environment.

Threats of school violence are unfortunate and all-too-common occurrences. Janel is certainly not alone in experiencing a cyber threat at her school. But the first time any teacher experiences any form of school violence, even with prior information and preparation, and even if it is a hoax, can be especially devastating and frightening. Today's schools are doing more to prepare teachers for all kinds of emergencies including active shooter training. And today's teachers must resist a culture of fear being promoted by those who would terrorize students and their families, teachers, and school personnel.

As we learn from Janel's situation, violence prevention is a full community effort that requires parental involvement and law enforcement in collaboration with the school. And schools need to be even more proactive in their efforts to respond to school emergencies, not offering training and information only after an incident has occurred. As stated on the Centers for Disease Control and Prevention (2016) webpage:

School violence can be prevented. Research shows that prevention efforts—by teachers, administrators, parents, community members, and even students—can reduce violence and improve the overall school environment. No one factor in isolation causes school violence, so stopping school violence involves using multiple prevention strategies that address the many individual, relationship, community, and societal factors that influence the likelihood of violence. Prevention efforts should ultimately reduce risk factors and promote protective factors at these multiple levels of influence. (para. 1)

Students and schedules are always going to be unpredictable; the spontaneous nature of the classroom is one of the reasons that so many of us love and
stay in this profession for so long. Being as prepared as possible, learning to
be flexible, considering multiple alternatives and making the best possible
choice (sometimes instantaneously), working cooperatively and collaboratively, and "doing everything you can do" are reassuring steps new teachers
can take in facing so many of the demands and surprises they encounter daily.
All three of Janel's situations demonstrate her development as an expert in
trusting her instincts, in ensuring the well-being of each of her students, and
in relying on experienced personnel for assistance and mentoring.

FOR DISCUSSION

1. School interruptions are a given, but Janel's narrative reminds us that there
   are different degrees of disruption, some more serious than others. In all
   three situations in her narrative, the administration intervened, and Janel
   cooperated with them to resolve these issues. What roles do you think the
   administration must or should play in their professional responsibilities to
   the teachers and the students?
2. Share and discuss drug, alcohol, or school violence prevention plans that
   you know about (e.g., D.A.R.E. America, lockdown drills) and whether or
   not you think that more should be done to address these areas in schools
   and why.

FOR REFLECTION

Janel offers two pieces of advice for beginning teachers, one is to have confidence, and the other is to let students know you care. Consider how you
would demonstrate these qualities in your own classroom and to what extent.

FOR INQUIRY

1. Research a health condition such as epilepsy, asthma, or a heart attack and
   what someone should do if a seizure or attack should occur in a public
   space.
2. Compare at least two disaster prevention or intervention plans from two
   different school districts and note the commonalities and differences in
   each. To what extent do you think these plans ensure the safety of school

personnel and students? If more should be done, what details would you add?

SUGGESTED READING

Centers for Disease Control and Prevention. (2016). School violence: Prevention. Retrieved from http://www.cdc.gov/violenceprevention/youthviolence/school violence/prevention.html.

Epilepsy Society. (2015). School, education, and epilepsy. Retrieved from https://www.epilepsysociety.org.uk/school-education-and-epilepsy#.WBjPGfRWJlc.

National Association of School Psychologists. (2015). School violence prevention. Retrieved from https://www.nasponline.org/resources-and-publications/resources/school-safety-and-crisis/school-violence-prevention.

National Center for Education in Maternal and Child Health. (2014). School violence prevention. Retrieved from http://www.ncemch.org/schools/violence.php.

Substance Abuse and Mental Health Services Administration. (2015). Underage drinking. Retrieved from http://www.samhsa.gov/underage-drinking-topic.

Chapter Fifteen

Defending and Protecting My Students

Caroline Lehman

Training that taught Caroline how to keep her students safe in the event of an attack has unintended consequences for her, triggering some soul-searching as she comes to grips with her role of protector.

It's now my fifth year of teaching and I've experienced fire drills, tornado drills, earthquake drills, and general lockdown drills, but ALICE (Alert, Lockdown, Inform, Counter, Evacuate) training has forced me to take a closer look at my role as protector and defender of my students.

ALICE training began as a morning in-service early in the fall. We had received a few e-mails that briefly explained what we were in for: the training would introduce protocols for what to do in the event of a violent intruder.

After the meeting that ended with the firing of blanks so we could "recognize the sound," I barely had enough time to walk to the middle school from the high school and set up the projector for the morning announcements before kids started pouring in. They bounded in, asking how my morning was going and what I learned about in the in-service. I told them that we were learning about school safety.

ALICE training continued throughout the school year. After some live drills with local law enforcement in the spring during which we practiced running, hiding, and fighting, we were asked to spend time in our rooms making escape plans. I went outside and determined that kids would need to jump on to a storage shed several feet below the windows and then jump to the ground. (We had been told that a broken arm or leg was better than losing a life.) I considered what it would take to break the window. Then I thought about my students—who might not be able to fit through the window or who might freeze in fear. In that case, what would I do?

I can't look at my classroom the same way now. Books are projectiles. Stashed shelves are barricade fodder. My cubbyholes under counters are no longer pockets for adolescent readers to squeeze into during independent reading time—they're shelters. Now every time I reach for the air freshener spray in the cabinet, I am reminded that I keep it there so I can spray it in an intruder's face.

I brought in an old field hockey stick and put it in my closet "just in case." I put my donated ladder under the window in a cabinet. I calculated exit strategies. And I wonder if I will be able to reach all of the weapons and tools in enough time to make a difference. My carefully constructed welcoming environment now seems a different place as I assess objects and think about how they can be used to save students' lives.

But ALICE training has not only made me think about and become familiar with strategies for keeping my students safe; it has also caused me to reflect on the potential that teaching has to help disturbed individuals—those individuals whose mental illnesses my cause them to engage in violent acts.

One of the greatest gifts I can give a student is what critic Kenneth Burke calls an "imaginative rehearsal" when the reader can explore and experience a situation or conflict in the safe, consequence-free space of the text. I know that fiction can provide windows into other perspectives and may foster empathy. Could richer reading lives prevent the kind of desensitization and detachment that individuals who initiate a school shooting possess?

Some studies suggest that the "Harry Potter Generation," that I am proud to lump myself into, is more aware of the dangers of prejudice from reading about the prejudicial treatment of muggles and mudbloods. I can give students choice in their reading and give them time to read and experience different worlds. I can show I'm interested in them as human beings and give them respect as I acknowledge their risks and challenges. Perhaps these endeavors, along with the strategies I've learned to keep them physically safe, will keep them emotionally safe, too.

Before you read Caroline's reflection and her concluding thoughts, jot down a few notes and/or questions that you have about what she has shared.

CAROLINE'S REFLECTION

In retrospect, I realize that most of my initial reactions and reflections were clearly tied to Danielson's Doman 2: The Classroom Environment. After focusing for so long on creating an open and welcoming physical space in my room, ALICE training directed me to reconsider Danielson's Component 2e: Organizing Physical Space to include how I might fortify and weaponize that same environment. Arranging my room for safety and accessibility now has another goal. Previously, I had considered ease of access, traffic flow, fostering a reading community, and the ability to use flexible grouping when considering the physical layout of my room. Now my air freshener spray is stored in the cabinet by the door instead of by my desk in case I need to use it to disarm and distract an active shooter.

While we were practicing barricading our door during a recent drill, administrators came around and jiggled our door handles. Even though I had practiced with our police department and staff, talked students through the process, and we were building a barricade at the moment, when I heard that handle jiggle, my world tilted, my heart leapt up, and real fear took my breath away. I knew it was a drill, but the drill was waking up those instincts that demanded I protect my students at all costs.

In that moment, I was acutely aware of my professional responsibility and role as teacher and mentor. I may have been experiencing anxiety, but it was important that students saw me making decisions and being confident about our actions. My sense of responsibility for maintaining my professionalism was strong as I dutifully participated in a safety initiative. The drills are difficult for me because I care about my students so much, but because I care I need to be open, honest, calm, and controlled when I share with students how I am processing these situations. They need to see me dealing with these drills as a human, but they also need to be reassured that I am in control and will do everything in my power to keep them safe.

What is clear to me now is how important it is for students to confront the idea of an unimaginable situation with their teacher present to help them process. I was hesitant and apprehensive about students joining our training. I was rattled enough as a teacher, so how would they react? Now that we've gone through some slow-motion live action drills during which students barricade and hide, I've been able to talk honestly with my students before, during, and after these drills. I admit that it scares me. I tell them that we hope this violence will never happen, but in the event of the unimaginable we want them to have choices, agency, and power.

I see the value in students undergoing and processing this training even if it is difficult to talk about. I hope that each time I practice drills with students that they can see me becoming more confident and sure of myself as their teacher, mentor, and protector. I hope that no emergency will force me to use ALICE training, but I am grateful that I am prepared to do so if necessary.

CAROLINE'S INTERVIEW WITH JO-ANNE

Caroline shared her final thoughts about her narrative and reflection in written responses to questions and in a face-to-face interview. When thinking about ALICE training she referred to Component 4f: Showing Professionalism, stating that one of her professional responsibilities is to be an advocate for her students. Knowing how important it is for students to be able to process these drills, when the first drill of the year was announced at a faculty meeting, Caroline inquired about the length of time given for the drills and if it included debriefing time to ensure that the drill included time for students to ask questions. She also makes sure that students know that the school psychologist and school counselors are available for them.

Further experience with and thinking about ALICE training and drills have led Caroline to the realization that she must continue to strive for an atmosphere of respect and rapport by "promoting acceptance and perspective taking in the texts that I choose and the way that my students communicate with others."

She also wonders how this kind of training is implemented in other schools; she knows how seriously she and her colleagues take the training; however, she believes that to "do it right is more than just following procedures . . . you need to anticipate how your students may react and also have the self-knowledge to know how to best approach it for yourself as well."

While initially shaken by ALICE training, Caroline now feels "more confident"—not only about her competence but also about how to frame this training for students. She tells students that the main goal of the training is to give them choices "to get themselves to safety" if the need arises, stating that "tension seems to be . . . removed from students when we focus on the fact that we have choices."

Caroline shared the experience of a recent live drill with students, during which they practiced barricading and evacuating. After building a barricade, Caroline and her students "sat on the floor in the dark" and she answered their questions and stated that she would do anything to protect them. When the door handle rattled, students' eyes widened, and she shared with them her own feelings (that she felt nervous but also felt a sense of agency) and complimented them on a job well done. Caroline believes that this conversation gave students a chance to "air their fears" and to see her "as a teacher, mentor, and protector."

Finally, Caroline shared her thinking about her role as "protector," a role that has become more visible as a result of the ALICE training. For her, the role of protector is part of who she is as a teacher. As protector, she also teaches students so that they understand the choices that they have in their lives—including choices of what to do in the case of an active shooter in their school.

JO-ANNE'S COMMENTARY

Parker Palmer (1998) reminds us that "education is a fearful enterprise" (p. 36), that both teachers and students are fearful, although the fear that he refers to is not related to school safety of the kind that Caroline has discussed; rather, he is looking at the fear that both teacher and students have that relate to teaching and learning.

Still, though, Palmer's thoughts on fear and its capacity to stultify teaching and learning are relevant, given the fear that Caroline experienced as a result of training that she was required to undergo and her understanding of a facet of her identity as a teacher that she had not previously considered: protector. For Caroline, safety and accessibility, an element of Component 2e: Organizing Physical Space, took on a much more serious consideration, as she notes the need to store her room freshener spray in a different place, as it is now a "weapon."

Palmer advocates that teachers make efforts to rid themselves of the "inner demons of fear" so that a "renewal of teaching and learning" can occur. For Caroline this meant coming to grips with her fears and anxieties through openness and honesty with her students. As noted throughout this collection, good teaching includes building and maintaining relationships with students. Caroline's relationship with her students was undermined by the fear that the ALICE training evoked. It wasn't until she was understood that she needed to talk candidly with her students about the training and her own anxieties, while also providing opportunity for students to share their fears and questions, that she was able to rein in her worries so that she could function fully in her role as teacher.

In her Foreword to Alsup's *Teacher Identity Discourses: Negotiating Personal and Professional Spaces* (2006), Deborah Britzman writes: "To know thyself is a paradox. It is to know that one must meet, again and again, the unknown other and, in doing so, the unknown self" (p. xii). We see in this assertion Caroline's experience discovering her responsibility as "protector" of her students, a responsibility that came to light when she began ALICE training. Caroline was forced to meet "an unknown other" and thus had to grapple with this newly discovered aspect of self, a struggle that weakened her relationship with her students until she was open and honest with them. Although this openness and honesty were designed to allay her students' concerns about safety, they also helped Caroline adjust to the role of protector.

Caroline's narrative and reflection demonstrate that the formation of a professional identity can be complicated by unanticipated institutional demands and professional expectations. The development of a teacher's professional identity is a complex, complicated process, necessitating a merging of the professional and personal (Alsup, 2006, p. xiv). Yet, integrating the personal self with professional responsibilities is no easy process. Alsup writes that "such a synergy involves bringing together, mixing and merging, and even welcoming a collision between personal ideologies and perceived professional responsibilities" (p. xiv).

Caroline's narrative certainly demonstrates this "mixing and merging" as well as a "collision between personal ideologies and perceived professional responsibilities." Her story also demonstrates the toll that this "mixing and merging" can take on a teacher's emotions and state of mind.

As a result of a spate of violent incidences in schools, a great deal of attention is being paid to ensuring that schools are safe and secure. For Caroline's school district, this attention included not only securing buildings but also training personnel and students. But this training had consequences that went beyond teachers and students learning how to conduct themselves during this type of event. For Caroline, the training precipitated anxiety and fear, as she reflected on her role as protector and her willingness to do anything to keep her students safe. Her fears and anxiety affected not only herself but also her relationship with her students—her rapport with her students.

Caroline's selflessness, her willingness to protect her students at all costs, highlights an interesting aspect of a teacher's identity, that is, successful teaching demands that teachers possess a firm sense of self. In other words, teachers must be both selfless and selfish, a "seemingly impossible seesaw to balance" (Alsup, 2006, p. 25).

Caroline's struggle, in part, was a result of her trying to achieve this balance—between her sense of self and her role of teacher-protector. She was working toward "self-actualization," a concept offered by Abraham Maslow (1962). Self-actualization includes an awareness of self and understanding of how the facets of one's self intersect. Caroline's story and reflection are a record of her reaching self-actualization, a state that then allows her to cope with her fears in productive ways while simultaneously serving her students by taking on the role of advocate.

Like Scott Gibbons' commentary and reflection in this collection, Caroline's narrative demonstrates the importance of care and of caring relationships in teachers' lives. Scott's students do well in his class because they know he cares about them. Caroline's students learned what to do to remain safe, however, they also learned that they could count on their teacher to act confidently and competently in the event of a violent incident, learning that occurred because Caroline manifested a caring attitude toward them, making a conscious effort to attend to their fears and also by acting with their best interests at heart—ensuring debriefing time and informing students about access to resources, such as the school psychologist and counselors.

Caroline's experience with ALICE training and its consequences provides corroboration for what Miller and Norris (2007) state about preservice teacher identity. It is "vulnerable to being co-constructed by competing agendas" at the same time as it is "predetermined because of institutional and social expectations" (Miller & Norris, 2007, pp. 21–22). The same thing can be said about the development of the novice teacher's professional identity. To some degree, the development of Caroline's professional identity was "predetermined," as she was expected to function as a protector after receiving requisite training.

The role of protector was given to Caroline and her colleagues; it was not sought by them, raising issues related to teacher agency. As defined by philosopher Michael Oakeshott (1975), agency is "the starting place of doing" (p. 32). Danielwicz (2001) expands on this definition of agency: "Agency can be defined as the power or freedom or will to act, to make decisions, to exert pressure, to participate . . . or to be strategically silent (p. 163).

While Caroline and her colleagues had no say in the decision to implement ALICE training, she was able to enact agency when she advocated for her students, ensuring debriefing time after drills. This agency was made possible because Caroline, in Oakeshott's (2001) view, had "an understanding of [herself] in terms of [her] wants and [her] powers" (p. 32). Part of becoming a professional, for Caroline, was recognizing and using her power to advocate for her students.

Caroline's story is a sobering reminder of a sad reality. School shootings and other violent acts in the school setting are rare, yet when one does occur, it elicits much attention. The school district in which Caroline teaches acted proactively, mandating training so that teachers and students would be well prepared for any violent incidences. However, as Caroline's narrative and reflection demonstrate, such training had unintended consequences that affected the construction of her professional identity and her relationship with her students.

FOR DISCUSSION

1. Return to the notes and questions you wrote before you read Caroline's reflection and final thoughts. What was your thinking at that point? What notes did you make? What questions did you have? How has your thinking changed? Were your questions answered?

2. Caroline explained how she worked to address her students' fears. What else might she have done to calm her students' fears?

FOR REFLECTION

The fear that Caroline experienced after the first training prevented her from having what Parker Palmer (1998) calls a "live encounter" with her students (p. 37). What might be some other reasons for a teacher avoiding a "live encounter" with his/her students? Have you ever had a teacher who avoided these "live encounters"? What effect did this avoidance have on the climate of the classroom and the teacher's rapport with students?

FOR INQUIRY

Survey some schools to find out what security and safety protocols are in place. Consider methods for admitting visitors, the use of metal detectors, the presence of security officers or police, security cameras, etc. Have teachers and staff received training for how to deal with an active shooter? What did this training consist of?

SUGGESTED READING

Keeping Candidates Safe: School Safety and Prevention of Violence for Pre-Service Teacher Education. (2016, October 30). Retrieved from https://www.pac-te.org/uploads/1384973438_PAC-TE%20School%20Safety%20Positon%20Paper%20Final%20Draft%20Oct%20%2024%2013.pdf.

May, D. C. (2014). *School safety in the United States: A reasoned look at the rhetoric.* Durham, NC: Carolina Academic Press.

Palmer, P. (1998). *The courage to teach: Exploring the inner landscape of a teacher's life.* San Francisco: Josey-Bass.

Afterword

Sarah Rhodes,
Linda Norris, and Jo-Anne Kerr

SARA'S REFLECTION

I have come to realize that there are areas of teaching for which I was very well prepared, especially Domain 1: Planning and Preparation, and Domain 3: Instruction. However, some components in Classroom Environment and Professionalism were not addressed; for example, Component 2c: "performance of non-instructional duties" and Component 4b "maintaining accurate non-instructional records." Also, while in methods courses we learned how to create lesson and unit plans, we did not learn how to adapt these plans in the case of unanticipated events that could affect implementation.

How planning must take into account the unpredictable nature of the learning environment was certainly demonstrated by my narrative. The cornerstone of my lesson was student-driven work on their essays using computers; the idea of the computers not working failed to enter my mind, so I had to do some quick thinking on my feet. But when planning, had I thought about how I could adapt if there was a problem with students using computers to produce their final drafts, I would not have been, at least momentarily, so panicked by the situation.

Thankfully, I came up with a solution to the dilemma. There was a computer lab next door that wasn't being used, so I sent students there. Luckily, I had knowledge of this school resource (Domain 1, Component 1d). Those students asking to use the restroom or go to their lockers? They were accommodated, although they were also told to hurry. What about my new student? A little later, I figured out how to meet his needs and also meet the research project requirement. The project had two components: an essay and a speech. I exempted him from one component of the project (the essay), while having

139

him complete the research and then incorporate this research into a presentation. He met, somewhat differently, the overall unit objective of learning how
to conduct and share the results of research.

Also, in the "conversation that started it all," Dr. Kerr and I discussed that
the non-instructional tasks (Component 2c) that are required of teachers are
not explained and discussed in methods courses, and we wanted to address
that gap. These are responsibilities that all teachers must fulfill, and many
student and novice teachers are overwhelmed when they realize how many
of them there are. More important, they are taken aback when these tasks
interfere with their carefully planned instruction.

I found that I was also overwhelmed by the many jobs for which I was
responsible and that ensured effective teaching and fulfillment of professional responsibilities, from taking attendance to making sure that handouts
were copied. I also struggled with these during student teaching. In response
to this struggle and others, my cooperating teacher developed a checklist (see
appendix B) that helped make these tasks more manageable for me.

As a result of my experience serving as a substitute teacher for seven
weeks, I learned to note in my unit plans how I might deal with a student who
enters class in the midst of a unit. Also, I include in lesson plans in which
technology is used an alternate plan in case the technology doesn't work or
isn't available. Preservice teachers can be directed to do the same things when
they are creating lesson and unit plans.

I also suggest integrating the non-instructional duties that are included in
Domain 2: Classroom Environment into lesson plans so that preservice teachers have a more accurate understanding of how lessons are implemented in
actual classrooms in which teachers not only teach the lesson but also take
attendance, write hall passes, return papers, and provide make up work to
students who have been absent, among other things.

JO-ANNE AND LINDA'S COMMENTARY

Sara's narrative is an appropriate set of "bookends" to frame the beginning
and ending of our text. Two aspects of Sara's narrative are key: 1) the struggles she contended with that day in the computer lab, from laptops not being
charged to the arrival of a new student at the end of a unit on research, are in
no way unique or atypical, and 2) Sara overcame these challenges with some
flexibility and with the adaptability that is essential to a strong pedagogical
foundation.

Sara's story foregrounds in rather dramatic fashion Danielson's Planning
and Preparation while simultaneously uncovering its complexities when

the vagaries of the learning environment interfere. As all the narratives in this collection show, these vagaries are manifold and range from unfortunate technology glitches to serious student concerns. However, a constant remains: the potential for these unpredictable, unanticipated occurrences is always present. Given this reality, then, what can teacher education programs do to prepare their candidates for the unpredictable and unanticipated?

Apparent in Sara's reflection and those of our contributors is an emergent way of thinking that is developing at the same time that a professional identity is being constructed. As noted in the introduction, to be useful for teachers, knowledge and skills must coexist with ways of thinking about teaching. Dispositional intelligence must be exercised—the predisposition to apply knowledge resulting from awareness that an opportunity is available to use the acquired learning (Tishman 2000, p. 49).

To implement the unit on research writing, Sara had to draw upon pedagogical content knowledge (knowledge and skills), however, this knowledge alone was insufficient when it bumped up against the realities of teaching—in this case, realities related to access to technology and a new student arriving without warning. Other realities interfered as well: students forgetting handouts and having to use the restroom. Thus, a perfect storm of sorts brewed, throwing Sara into momentary panic. While ultimately she dealt with this perfect storm with good sense, she realizes in retrospect how she could have mitigated the situation somewhat before it occurred.

Sara's stint as a substitute teacher provided opportunity for her to develop a way of thinking like a teacher that would help her navigate her way through the complexities of teaching; she was in the process of constructing a professional identity, not only enacting best practice but also contending with the daily ins and outs of teaching. A substitute teacher but also a novice teacher, Sara was nonetheless expected to be an expert, given that she had been hired to fill a position. Yet, as she makes clear in her story, she was still learning how to function in the role of teacher; in other words, while perceived as "expert," she was in the early stages of forging a professional identity, one aspect of which was learning how to think like a teacher.

What becomes apparent, then, through close examination and analysis of Sara's narrative is that educator preparation programs must attend to the development of professional dispositions and must make explicit how professional identities are constructed and coconstructed, to foreground the transition from instructional consumer to instructional leader that teacher candidates must navigate, something that this collection strives to do.

Sara notes that during student teaching she struggled with fulfilling routine responsibilities, so much so that her cooperating teacher devised a checklist to assist her (see appendix B). As the checklist demonstrates, these responsibilities are necessary for effective teaching while indicating the complexity inherent in teaching, for in addition to routine tasks, teachers must also complete other demanding duties, such as planning and implementing lessons and putting to use pedagogical content knowledge.

In *The Checklist Manifesto: How to Get Things Right* (2009), Atul Gawande characterizes checklists as quick and simple tools for boosting the skills of experts. Gawande notes that checklists are "protection against failure" and that they also instill a kind of discipline of higher performance. This protection against failure is especially necessary in complex environments, such as a classroom.

A look at the checklist that Sara's cooperating teacher created confirms this function; if followed, the items will protect against failure while simultaneously fostering a kind of discipline of higher performance. The checklist encapsulates key aspects of effective teaching and illustrates what Gawande shares about good checklists; they are "precise . . . efficient, to the point, and easy to use even in . . . difficult situations." They are "reminders of only the most critical and important steps" (2009, p. 120).

Sara's checklist, or a modified version of it, can be used in methods courses to help teacher candidates begin to understand the complexities of the teaching and learning environment. Such a checklist will also encourage ways of thinking that will augment the pedagogical content knowledge that teacher candidates are amassing in these courses, a primary goal, as strong pedagogical content knowledge is often insufficient in the real world of teaching when technology fails or is unavailable, when a 45 minute period is cut short by an unforeseen early dismissal, or when a student is in distress and needs a teacher's empathy and understanding before class begins.

Both Alsup (2006) and Darling-Hammond (2006) allude to the complexity of teaching, complexity usually not shared with teacher candidates. Lampert (2001) explains that one of the reasons for this complexity results from the fact that the problems that teachers face occur at the same time so that "different problems must be addressed in a single action" and that this action also involves interaction with students individually and in groups (p. 2).

We see this complexity play out in Sara's story. She had to devise a way that students could word process their research papers, deal with students' requests to use the restroom and go to lockers to retrieve forgotten materials, and, finally, welcome a new student, all at the same time. However, we then recognize in her reflection an emerging way of thinking that can be used to manage this complexity, as she understands the need to plan to the best of her ability for the unexpected.

CONCLUDING THOUGHTS FROM LINDA AND JO-ANNE

In the film *Sully* (2016), Tom Hanks portrays the American Airlines pilot who has to make several split-second decisions after his aircraft has been compromised by a bird strike. In about 37 seconds, Captain Chesley Sullenberger must put all of his previous expertise as a pilot to the ultimate test of survival for himself, his crew, and his precious cargo. The decision he makes to land the plane in the Hudson River seems almost automatic for this seasoned veteran of the air.

This movie parallels, perhaps a bit more theatrically, some key points of this text. This film, our text, and the many sources and resources we have referenced throughout help us to recognize that spontaneous decisionmaking, weighing options, and making the right choices come with lots of practice and experience. Expert teaching is, in fact, achieved mainly through lived experience and knowledge acquisition, just as in expert piloting or gaining expertise in nursing, acting, and many other professions.

Diane Ravitch (2016) notes in her study of the American school system that "Goldhaber and Hansen found that consistency of job performance and productivity became greater as teacher become more experienced" (p. 196); in the same study, Ravich also refers to a 2006 paper by Gordon, Kane, and Staiger who argued that "differences between 'stronger teachers' and 'weaker teachers' become clear only after teachers had been teaching for a couple of years" (p. 192).

Years of classroom experience definitely contribute to the knowledge, skills, and dispositions necessary to think like an expert; but we believe that mentoring new candidates by discussing how both novices and experts respond to specific situations and teaching new candidates to be physically, mentally, and emotionally aware of their surroundings and to be highly reflective of their thoughts, words, and actions can go a long way to create an earlier sense of expertise in neophyte teachers.

Because the nature of schooling is always unpredictable, and some school situations can be dangerous and life-threatening, the better we can mentor new teachers to think on their feet and to choose competently, guided by critical thinking about what is the best choice at that time and in that space, the better it will be for their charges as well.

In our introduction we assert the power of story to tell truths about teaching, and we affirm and validate novice teachers' voices to offer insightful glimpses into the real world of teaching in a quest to help teacher candidates and novice teachers become more effective practitioners by providing earlier opportunities to identify and analyze professional dispositions. The development of ways of thinking like a more experienced teacher is key to successful teaching, seeing this development as part of the construction of a professional identity. While we acknowledge the complicated, complex nature of teaching, we also offer a way to conceptualize and make sense of this work by using Danielson's Framework.

Taken together, the narratives we have shared provide a rich, even daunting, picture of teaching; separately they tease out the innumerable challenges that teachers contend with on a daily basis. Acknowledging these challenges is imperative; providing opportunity for teacher candidates and novice teachers to identify and consider how to meet these challenges successfully is equally imperative. We believe that with more conscious and conscientious practice, including working alongside informed professional personnel at the school and university levels, new teachers can begin to emulate expert teacher behaviors earlier and experience more success in the classroom.

We must also do a better job of assisting teacher candidates and new teachers in understanding what resources, in and outside of their schools, are available to them, where they can be found, and when each is most useful and appropriate. In *Reign of Error* (2014) Diane Ravitch reminds us that in order to strengthen the whole teaching profession, we must "Insist that teachers, principals, and superintendents be professional educators" (p. 274); she provides very clear guidelines for the qualifications professionals must meet in order to cultivate thriving schools including that teachers "should deepen their knowledge of the subject they plan to teach with opportunities to plan lessons and work with mentors" (p. 275).

The cliché, "It takes a village to raise a child" seems applicable here. Certainly, the responsibility for any person's education and educational well-being cannot rest with just one individual, especially a first-year teacher.

Looking back on what these teachers wrote and said, we marvel at how they retained and applied what they learned from our secondary undergraduate and graduate English programs to the new territories they entered; we are in awe at their passion and love for students and schooling. And we are humbled at their willingness to share what happened to them on a day-to-day basis, how hard they tried to be successful for their students, and at how much they learned from reviewing the choices they made and what they might do if in a similar situation.

Their stories prompted us to tell some of our own stories relevant to their circumstances; perhaps our readers felt themselves nodding in agreement as we did, thinking, yes, I remember this, or something very similar happened in my classroom. These stories have helped us as teacher educators to know much more about what we need to do in our methods classes to prepare future teachers for the field; through the analysis of each story, we were able to raise new questions that could be discussed and responded to in and outside of our classrooms and find new resources and new strategies to pass on to them for future reference.

Their narratives reminded us of the power of storytelling and how we at a very early age desire to be told stories of all kinds because that is one of the essential ways humans communicate, learn about their cultures, and relate to one another. What we have tried to create here is similar to what Dyson and Genishi (1994) called for in their idea of "Community Writing as a Cultural Forum." They advocate "sharing life experiences and telling 'mirror stories' that lead to the breaking of silences, boosting identity and self-esteem, raising consciousness and political awareness, sharing information and resources, bonding and building an internal community, pure and simple teaching and learning, and supporting each other to take action in the world" (Dyson & Genishi, 1994, p. 225).

We hope this work will assist new teachers in new ways of thinking about their calling, for example, recognizing that there is not just a single choice about what to do in a given situation, that they can remain calm and act professionally as role models for their students, they can rely on many personnel including their cooperating teacher, administration, and community for assistance, that they can use tools like checklists and technology to enhance teaching excellence.

The new teachers in our study have reminded us that each day the classroom offers new challenges, situations, dilemmas, frustrations, and problems to solve. All sixteen teachers tackled their dilemmas head-on and got through the day. They used their energy, enthusiasm, empathy, subject matter knowledge, pedagogical knowledge, physical, mental, and emotional resources to work it out. Later, they used critical reflection to learn what they might do differently or better next time. They grew from the experience. That is what experts do. They have helped us to define situational pedagogy to a greater extent and to realize that providing specific situational pedagogy examples to teacher candidates may assist them in thinking more critically and more expertly earlier in their teaching careers. That is our contribution from this project.

What is not in this book is the impossible task of sharing the hundreds of other stories new teachers tell us every day. But we do hope others will come forward and share more situational narratives in the future—happy and sad, scary and surprising, and real. The daily joys of teaching, the power of literacy learning for young people, the sheer excitement of not knowing exactly what each new day will bring, the flexibility and spontaneity, the resilience of our students, the 80 percent or more who come to school each day, prepared, eager, and wanting to learn are just some of the reasons we have so loved being in this profession.

Finally, we assert that the ability and predisposition to think like a more expert teacher is especially imperative today given the challenges to the profession and public education. The ability to think like an experienced teacher assures effective, student-centered teaching but also predisposes newer teachers to articulate their beliefs about teaching to a wider audience and thus to function as advocates for students as well as for the profession.

Appendix A

Thinking Like a Teacher: *Stage 2 Reflecting on Narratives and Danielson's Framework for Teaching*

For this stage of your work, we would like you to reflect on the story that you shared in light of Charlotte Danielson's "Framework for Teaching" (2007, pp. 2–3). As you reconsider the experience you shared in your narrative, you may ask yourself these questions:

- What are you noticing as you consider your story in light of one of Danielson's domains?
- What new insights have emerged for you from your re-examination?
- What might you have done differently now that you have evolved as a practitioner?
- What is clear to you now that wasn't clear at the time of the experience that you shared?

Please begin your reflection with this statement: "After writing my story and thinking about it again with Danielson's Framework in mind, I realize . . ."

Please e-mail your reflection to Jo-Anne as an attachment by February 1.

Appendix A

Danielson's Domains, Components, and Elements of the Framework for Teaching

Domain 1: Planning and Preparation	*Domain 2: The Classroom Environment*
Component 1a: Demonstrating Knowledge of Content and Pedagogy • Knowledge of content and the structure of the discipline • Knowledge of prerequisite relationships • Knowledge of content-related pedagogy *Component 1b: Demonstrating Knowledge of Students* • Knowledge of child and adolescent development • Knowledge of the learning process • Knowledge of students' skills, knowledge, and language proficiency • Knowledge of students' interests and cultural heritage • Knowledge of students' special needs *Component 1c: Setting Instructional Outcomes* • Value, sequence, and alignment • Clarity • Balance • Suitability for diverse learners *Component 1d: Demonstrating Knowledge of Resources* • Resources for classroom use • Resources to extend content knowledge and pedagogy • Resources for students *Component 1e: Designing Coherent Instruction* • Learning activities • Instructional materials and resources • Instructional groups • Lesson and unit structure *Component 1f: Designing Student Assessments* • Congruence with instructional outcomes • Criteria and standards • Design of formative assessments • Use for planning	*Component 2a: Creating an Environment of Respect and Rapport* • Teacher interaction with students • Student interaction with other students *Component 2b: Establishing a Culture for Learning* • Importance of the content • Expectations for learning and achievement • Student pride in work *Component 2c: Managing Classroom Procedures* • Management of instructional groups • Management of transitions • Management of materials and supplies • Performance of non-instructional duties • Supervision of volunteers and paraprofessionals *Component 2d: Managing Student Behavior* • Expectations • Monitoring of student behavior • Response to student misbehavior *Component 2e: Organizing Physical Space* Safety and accessibility • Arrangement of furniture and use of physical resources

Domain 3: Instruction	Domain 4: Professional Responsibilities
Component 3a: Communicating with Students • Expectations for learning • Directions and procedures • Explanation of content • Use of oral and written language *Component 3b: Using Questioning and Discussion Techniques* • Quality of questions • Discussion techniques • Student participation *Component 3c: Engaging Students in Learning* • Activities and assignments • Grouping of students • Instructional materials and resources • Structure and pacing *Component 3d: Using Assessment in Instruction* • Assessment criteria • Monitoring of student learning • Feedback to students • Student self-assessment and monitoring of progress *Component 3e: Demonstrating Flexibility and Responsiveness* • Lesson adjustment • Response to students • Persistence	*Component 4a: Reflecting on Teaching* • Accuracy • Use in future teaching *Component 4b: Maintaining Accurate Records* • Student completion of assignments • Student progress in learning • Non-instructional records *Component 4c: Communicating with Families* • Information about the instructional program • Information about individual students • Engagement of families in the instructional program *Component 4d: Participating in a Professional Community* • Relationship with colleagues • Involvement in a culture of professional inquiry • Service to the school • Participation in school and district projects *Component 4e: Growing and Developing Professionally* • Enhancement of content knowledge and pedagogical skill • Receptivity to feedback from colleagues • Service to the profession *Component 4f: Showing Professionalism* • Integrity and ethical conduct • Service to students • Advocacy • Decision making • Compliance with school and district regulations

Appendix B
New Teacher Checklist

Preparation and Organization	☐ All material prepared and ready to go before students arrive (e.g., handouts are readily available; projector turned on; visual aids ready to go on the computer). ☐ Research background information on material being taught. ☐ Proofread all handouts, visual aids, etc. ☐ Classroom neat and organized. ☐ Plan in place for make up work for absent students. ☐ Consistent contact with special education teacher.
Lesson Planning	☐ Turn in lessons a week in advance of teaching along with supplemental materials. ☐ Backward design: plan assessments first and then instruction. ☐ Include unit and lesson essential questions that are aligned with standards. ☐ Introductions and conclusions for lessons. ☐ Generate creative activities to engage students and that meet standards.
Instruction	☐ Clearly explain directions, assignments, tasks, projects, examples, etc. ☐ Model correct grammar and usage. ☐ Include clear introductions and conclusions for lessons. ☐ Guide students in discovering essential information, as opposed to telling them. ☐ Assess what students are learning throughout lesson/unit and adjust instruction as needed. ☐ Ensure that all students are participating or are being engaged in the lesson. ☐ Incorporate technology on a regular basis. ☐ Present lessons in an organized, coherent manner. ☐ Ask engaging questions that lead to higher-level thinking. ☐ Prompt and rephrase questions as needed.

Content Knowledge	☐ Understand material being taught; convey it to students in a way that they will understand. ☐ Decide what is important for students to take away from each unit. ☐ Make real-world connections to content.
Classroom Management	☐ Maintain a mutually respectful environment. ☐ Keep all students on task. ☐ Avoid being taken advantage of by students who try to get away with things (sitting where they want, leaving the room often, talking when they shouldn't be, etc.). ☐ Maintain contact with parents. ☐ Be consistent with classroom rules, late/make up work policy, etc.
Pacing	☐ Allow an appropriate amount of time for completion of assignments. ☐ Be willing to adjust time frames if necessary, without giving into unwarranted student complaints.
Grading	☐ Grade fairly and precisely. Make accurate marks and comments on writing. ☐ Create rubrics that reflect standards and unit and lesson essential questions. ☐ Assign appropriate amounts of work and points for each level at any given time.
Voice	☐ Use a tone of voice appropriate to each situation.
Multitasking	☐ Work with one students while maintaining order with the rest of the class. ☐ During direct instruction, answer questions while staying on task with instruction. ☐ Collect papers, return papers, assign work, etc., in an efficient manner without taking away from class time or becoming distracted.

Note. We are grateful to Jessica Smith, Brookville Area High School, Brookville, Pennsylvania, for allowing us to share this checklist with our readers.

References

ALICE Training Institute. (2013–2016). Retrieved from https://www.alicetraining.com.

Alsup, J. (2006). *Teacher identity discourses: Negotiating personal and professional spaces.* Mahwah, NJ: Lawrence Erlbaum.

Balfanz, R., & Byrnes, V. (2012). The importance of being in school: A report on absenteeism in the nation's public schools. Johns Hopkins University. School of Education. Retrieved from http://new.every1graduates.org/wp-content/uploads/2012/05/FINALChronicAbsenteeismReport_May16.pdf.

Britzman, D. P. (2003). *Practice makes practice: A critical study of learning to teach.* Albany: State University of New York Press.

Burden, P. (2012). *Classroom management: Creating a successful K–12 learning community.* 5th ed. Hoboken, NJ: John Wiley & Sons.

Burke, J. (2010). *What's the big idea? Question-driven units to motivate reading, writing, and thinking.* Portsmouth, NH: Heinemann.

Burke, J., with Krajicek, J. (2006). *Jim Burke's letters to a new teacher: A month-by-month guide to the year ahead.* Portsmouth, NH: Heinemann.

A call for more effective prevention of violence. (2012, December 19). Retrieved from http://curry.virginia.edu/articles/sandyhookshooting.

Centers for Disease Control and Prevention. (2016). School violence: Prevention. Retrieved from http://www.cdc.gov/violenceprevention/youthviolence/school violence/prevention.html

Christel, M. T., & Sullivan, S. (Eds.). (2007). *Lesson plans for creating media-rich classrooms.* Urbana, IL: NCTE.

Danielson, C. (2007). *Enhancing professional practice: A framework for teaching.* Alexandria, VA: Association for Supervision and Curriculum Development.

Danielwicz, J. P. (2001). *Teaching selves: Identity, pedagogy, and teacher education.* Albany: State University of New York Press.

Darling-Hammond, L. (2006). *Powerful teacher education: Lessons from exemplary programs.* San Francisco: Jossey-Bass.

Dewey, J. (1977). Essays on the new empiricism. In J. Boydston (Ed.), *The middle works of John Dewey.* Vol. 3: *1899–1924.* Carbondale: Southern Illinois University Press.

Dyson, A., & Genishi, C. (Eds.). (1994). The need for story: Cultural diversity in classroom and community. Urbana, IL: NCTE.

The educational theory of Nel Noddings. (2011). New Foundations. Retrieved from http://www.newfoundations.com/GALLERY/Noddings.html.

Epilepsy and your child's school. (2016). WebMD. Retrieved from http://www.webmd.com/epilepsy/guide/children-school.

Fecho, B., Falter, M., & Hong, X. (Eds.). (2016). *Teaching outside the box but inside the standards: Making room for dialogue.* New York: Teachers College Press.

Flanagan, S. & Shoffner, M. (2016). *Teaching with(out) technology: Secondary English teachers and classroom technology use.* Retrieved from http://www.citejournal.org/volume-13/issue-3-13/general/teaching-without-technology-secondary-english-teachers-and-classroom-technology-use/.

Gawande, A. (2009). *The checklist manifesto: How to get things rights.* New York: Metropolitan Books.

Gere, A. R., Fairbanks, A. H., Roop, L., & Schaafsma, D. (1992). *Language and reflection: An integrated approach to teaching English.* New York: Macmillan.

Goldhaber, D. & Hansen, M. (2008). *Assessing the potential of using value-added estimates of teacher job performance for making tenure decisions.* Washington, D.C.: CALDER, Urban Institute.

Gordon, R., Kane, T. J., & Staiger, D.O. (2006). Identifying effective teachers using performance on the job. Discussion Paper. Washington. D.C.: Brookings Institution.

Houguet. D. (2016, September 21). How we can responsibly talk to children about suicide. Retrieved from https://www.nami.org/Blogs/NAMI-Blog/September-2016/How-We-Can-Responsibly-Talk-to-Children-About-Suic#sthash.fd9daIHV.dpuf.

Kajder, S. (2010). *Adolescents and digital literacies.* Urbana, IL: NCTE.

Kounin, J. S. (1970). *Discipline and group management in classrooms.* Huntington, NY: Holt, Rinehart and Winston.

Lampert, M. (2001). *Teaching problems and the problems of teaching.* New Haven: Yale University Press.

MacNeal, L. (1986). *Contradictions of control: School structure and school knowledge.* New York: Routledge and Kegan Paul.

Maslow, A. (1962). *Toward a psychology of being.* New York: Van Nostrand.

McCann, T. M., Johannessen, L. R., Kahn, E., & Flanagan, J. M. (2006). *Talking in class: Using discussion to enhance teaching and learning.* Urbana, IL: NCTE.

McCutcheon, G. (1992). Facilitating teacher personal theorizing. In E.W. Ross, J. W. Cornett, and G. McCutcheon (Eds.), *Teacher personal theorizing* (pp. 191–206). Albany: State University of New York Press.

Miller, sj, & Norris, L. (2007). *Unpacking the loaded teacher matrix: Negotiating space and time between university and secondary English classrooms.* New York: Peter Lang.

NAMI: National Alliance on Mental Illness. (2016). Retrieved from https://www
.nami.org/About-NAMI.

National Association of School Psychologists. (2015). Responding to school violence:
Tips for administrators. Retrieved from https://www.nasponline.org/resources-
and-publications/resources/school-safety-and-crisis/school-violence-prevention/
responding-to-school-violence-tips-for-administrators.

Noddings, N. (1992). *The challenge to care in schools: An alternative approach to
education.* New York: Teachers College Press.

Oakeshott, M. (1975). *On human conduct.* Oxford: Oxford University Press.

PA-ETEP. (2017). Retrieved from https://paetep.net.

PAC-TE School Safety and the Prevention of Violence Committee. (2016). Retrieved from https://www.pac-te.org/member-school-safety-and-the-prevention-of-
violence.

Palmer, P. J. (1998). *The courage to teach: Exploring the inner landscape of a
teacher's life.* San Francisco: Jossey-Bass.

Pennsylvania Department of Education. Standards Aligned System. (2017). Retrieved
from https://www.pdesas.org.

Pennsylvania Department of Human Services. Childline abuse registry. (2017).
Retrieved from http://www.dhs.pa.gov/provider/childwelfareservices/childlineand
abuseregistry/

Pennsylvania Family Support Alliance. Who are mandated reporters? (2017).
Retrieved from http://www.pa-fsa.org/Mandated-Reporters/Understanding-Man
dated-Reporting/Frequently-Asked-Questions.

Pennsylvania Professional Standards and Practices Commission. Code of professional practice and conduct for educators. (2017). Retrieved from www.pspc
.education.pa.gov/Statutes-Regulations-Policies-Forms/Code-of-Professional-
Practice-Conduct/Pages/default.aspx

Proto, M. (2013). *Teacher "Withithess."* Retrieved from https://quschoolofeducation
.wordpress.com/2013/10/07/teacher-withitness/.

Ravitch, D. (2014). *Reign of error: The hoax of the privatization movement and the
danger to America's public schools.* New York: Alfred A. Knopf.

Ravitch, D. (2016). *The death and life of the great American school system: How testing and choice are undermining education.* New York: Basic Books.

Sapon-Shevin, M. (2010). *Because we can change the world: A practical guide to
building cooperative, inclusive classroom communities.* Thousand Oaks, CA:
Corwin.

Smith, M. K. (2016). Nel Noddings, the ethics of care and education. *The encyclo-
paedia of informal education.* Retrieved from http://infed.org/mobi/nel-noddings-
the-ethics-of-care-and-education/.

Smith, M. W., & Wilhelm, J. D. (2002). *Reading don't fix no Chevys: Literacy in the
lives of young men.* Portsmouth, NH: Heinemann.

Substance Abuse and Mental Health Services Administration. (2015). Underage
drinking. Retrieved from http://www.samhsa.gov/underage-drinking-topic.

Sully. (2016). Clint Eastwood, Director/Producer. Warner Bros. and Village Road-
show Pictures.

Tishman, S. (2000). Why teach habits of mind? In A. L. Costa & B. Kailick (Eds.), Discovering and exploring habits of mind (pp. 41–52). Alexandria, VA: Association for Supervision and Curriculum Development.

Tishman, S. Jay, E., & Perkins, D. N. (1992). Teaching thinking dispositions: From transmission to enculturation. Retrieved from http://citeseerx.ist.psu.edu/viewdoc/download;jsessionid=1CDBD770FAA1879FFE8A3418FC57E4A4?doi=10.1.1.23.7880&rep=rep1&type=pdf.

Vaznis, J. (2016). Schools struggle to cope with rising mental health needs. (2016, May 17). Boston Globe. Retrieved from https://www.bostonglobe.com/metro/2016/05/16/schools-confront-students-rising-mental-health-toll/J4nGkaSY-W23qDbmQ2PmjLO/story.html.

Yacapsin, M. (2011). Self-care for the student teacher: A promising new practice for teacher education programs. *Pennsylvania Teacher Educator, 10*, 1 19.

Index

NCTE (see National Council of
Teachers of English)
Nettles, D., 58
No Child Left Behind Act, 109
Noddings, N., 43, 45, 56, 154, 155
Norris, L., xx, xxv, xxxiii, 23, 24, 25,
118, 137, 154, 163

Oakeshott, M., 137
objectives, learning, 28, 29, 33, 41, 49,
90, 91, 104, 105, 107, 108
observation, of teaching, 3, 4, 5, 6, 7, 8

PAC-TE (see Pennsylvania Association
of Colleges and Teacher Educators)
Palmer, P., 24, 26, 45, 135, 138, 155
parents: and student absenteeism, 78,
79, 80, 82, 83, 84; communication
with, 20, 21, 23, 55, 152; demands,
expectations of, 24, 25, 56, 74, 125;
involvement with school, xxxi, 19, 20,
22, 49, 50, 51, 80, 95, 96, 98, 128
parenting, academic, 98
pedagogy, xix, xxix, 1, 16, 43, 44, 51,
71, 148
pedagogy, situational, xx, xxiii, xxviii,
145
Pennsylvania: Code of Professional
Practices and Conduct for Educators,
100; Department of Education, xviii,
xxxiii, 8; Department of Education
Standards Aligned System, 8;
Department of Human Services, 100;
Electronic Teacher Evaluation Portal,
8; Family Support Alliance, 100
Pennsylvania Association of Colleges
and Teacher Educators, xxxiii, 116,
117, 118, 155, 163
Perkins, D.N., xxiii, xxxiii, 141, 155
personnel, school, technical, university,
30, 31, 98, 99, 100 127, 128, 129,
130, 136, 144, 145
phonics, teaching of, 69, 72, 73, 75
planning and preparation, xiii, xxix,
xxxi, 6, 24, 25, 43, 53, 70, 72, 79

planning period, 19, 20, 21, 22
Plan of Improvement, 8
Principal, building: as evaluator, xxix, 3,
4, 5, 6, 7, 8; teachers' relationships
with, 7, 9, 21, 22; responsibilities of,
9, 21, 23, 77, 83, 97, 122, 125, 128,
144
Prinkey, J. vii, xxxi, 121, 158
professional: community, 72, 73, 111,
117; conversation, xxvii, xxviii;
development, 49, 54, 56, 74, 82, 166;
dispositions, xv, xxiii, 141, 143, 144;
expectations, x, 115, 136; identity, x,
xix, xxi, xxv, xxix, xxxi, xxxii, 6, 7,
15, 23, 44, 69, 124, 136, 137, 141;
relationships; responsibilities, xxxi,
xxxii, 23, 44, 45, 53, 73, 83, 123,
129, 133, 134, 140, 144; services,
115; stress and compassion fatigue
of, 100
professional identity, growth and
development of, 5, 7, 15, 73, 124,
137
professionalism, xxix, 22, 23, 70, 98,
107, 133
Proto, M., 91, 92, 155

Radiolab, 4
rapport: among students, 42, 43;
classroom, 37, 41; creating,
establishing, vii, xxx, xxxi, 39,
40, 41, 43, 44, 45, 56, 79, 81, 89,
97, 108, 115; environment of, 40,
43, 96, 98, 134; teachers' with
administrators, 22, 23; teachers' with
students, 22, 39, 40, 41, 42, 43, 55,
56, 72, 99, 101, 105, 106, 136, 138
Raths J.D., xxiii, xxxiii
Ravitch, D., 143, 144 155
ReadWriteThink, 4
reflection: as habit of mind, xxiv, 24;
as disposition, xxiv; assignments,
8; authentic, xxii; For Reflection
assignments, xxviii, 9, 18, 25, 34, 57,
66, 75, 85, 91, 101, 109, 118 129,

About the Editors and Contributors

ABOUT THE EDITORS

Dr. Jo-Anne Kerr taught high school English for twenty-five years and is now Professor of English at Indiana University of Pennsylvania where she teaches English and English education methods courses and supervises student teachers. Jo-Anne is director of IUP's English Education Program and has received the Outstanding Advisor Award multiple times from the IUP English  Department. She serves as the managing editor of the *Pennsylvania Teacher Educator* journal.

 **Dr. Linda Norris** taught secondary English for more than fifteen years and is Professor of English at IUP where she has taught English, secondary English teacher preparation, and supervised student teachers for the past twenty-four years. Linda received the 2007 Richard A. Meade Award from the National Council of Teachers of English and the 2009 Pennsylvania Teacher Educator of the Year Award from the Pennsylvania Association of Colleges and Teacher Educators. She serves as editor of the *Pennsylvania Teacher Educator* journal.

ABOUT THE CONTRIBUTORS

Tara Brodish graduated from Indiana University of Pennsylvania in 2012 with a bachelor of science degree in English education. After graduation Tara added teaching certifications in art and family and consumer sciences. She has been teaching art at the middle and high schools in the Windber Area School District (Winder, Pennsylvania) since 2013. In 2016, Tara earned a master's degree in adult and community Education. Tara chose to work in the field of education because she has an affinity for working with and  for others while developing relationships and utilizing those relationships to effect change. Tara values a strong educational foundation because she understands the importance education plays in a successful democratic society. She also really likes school supplies.

 **Shane Conrad** is an Indiana University of Pennsylvania alumnus, having earned a bachelor of science degree in English education in 2012. Shane was also valedictorian of his class. He received a master's degree in education and communication from the University of Pittsburgh in 2014. Shane is now teaching seventh grade humanities at the Monarch Global Academy, a charter school that is part of the Anne Arundale County Public Schools. When he's not grading papers or planning lessons, which is rare, he enjoys cycling, fitness activities, and reading young adult fiction. Shane hopes to one day take his career into the post-secondary world to help impart the lessons he has learned to bright young minds like the ones currently holding this book. He is married and lives in Washington, D.C.

Richard Courtot transferred to Indiana University of Pennsylvania from Wilkes University in 2010, where he studied English education and philosophy. He graduated in 2014 with bachelor of science degree in English education and a minor in philosophy. Shortly after graduating, Ricky moved to Montgomery County, Maryland, and began working as a substitute teacher in the Montgomery County Public School System. At the end of his first school year as a substitute, he was hired

as a full-time seventh grade English teacher at Gaithersburg Middle School. He is now in his third year at Gaithersburg Middle School, where he teaches eighth grade English.

Ian Cunningham is a 2012 graduate of Indiana University of Pennsylvania. He holds teaching certifications in English and English as a second language and works for the Greater Johnstown School District in Johnstown, Pennsylvania, teaching seventh grade English language arts. Hailing from a long familial line of storytellers, Ian developed an understanding of the importance of refined speaking and writing at a young age and set his sights on a career in English education when he was a mischievous middle schooler. It is with both irony and understanding that he now works with the middle school population. In the classroom, Ian focuses on developing literacy across all avenues of communication to promote problem solving, critical research, and evidentiary reasoning skills among his students. Outside of the classroom, he's normally hiding in the woods (often with a book) hunting or fishing.

Samantha DiMauro was born in Brooklyn, New York, and grew up in Gaithersburg, Maryland. She earned an associate's degree from Montgomery College in 2008. She earned a bachelor of arts degree in English from Indiana University of Pennsylvania in May 2012 and a master's degree in teaching English in December 2014. Samantha is currently working on a M Ed in literacy at IUP with reading specialist certification. She is also working as an adjunct instructor, teaching English at a community college.

Emily DuPlessis graduated from Indiana University of Pennsylvania with a bachelor of science degree in English education. After graduation Emily began her career teaching English at a high school in suburban Northern Virginia. While teaching in Northern Virginia, she earned her master's degree in English with a concentration in linguistics and her T.E.S.L. certificate from George Mason University. Emily currently teaches middle school reading and is an instructional coach Marion Center High School in western Pennsylvania. In her instructional coach role, she attends professional development workshops throughout the state and shares new strategies and technologies with colleagues in one-on-one and small group settings. Emily also works in conjunction with the administrative team to analyze data and to plan and implement building wide initiatives. Her continued dedication to the field of education is apparent in her collaboration with others to present at local and national conferences.

Nicole Frankenfield graduated from Indiana University of Pennsylvania in 2013 with a bachelor of science degree in English education. After graduation, Nicole was offered a position teaching English language arts for a school district in West Virginia. Currently, Nicole teaches seventh grade reading and language in the Springfield School District in Martinsburg, West Virginia. In addition to teaching and learning, she enjoys reading good stories, spending time with family, and serving in her church and community. She lives in Carlisle, Pennsylvania, with her husband and daughter.

Patrick Gahagan earned a bachelor of science degree in English education from Indiana University of Pennsylvania in 2015. Since then Pat has worked as an SAT tutor and a gymnastics coach, both of which have allowed him to apply many instructional strategies learned during in his program of study. Since his mother's death in 2016, Pat has found new inspiration

in a different field of study. He hopes to be accepted into medical school or a physician's assistant program. During his mother's battle with cancer, he was her health care advocate and had the opportunity to interact with some talented healthcare professionals. Pat decided to become a teacher because he wanted to help people reach their highest potential and better themselves. Now he hopes to help people in a different way.

Scott Gibbons graduated from Indiana University of Pennsylvania in 2005, where he earned a bachelor of science degree in English education. After graduation Scott taught high school English language arts for eleven years, four years in Pennsylvania and seven years in Kentucky. Scott is currently a doctoral student in the Educational Studies Program at the University of Cincinnati.

Teaching has always been his passion, and after receiving his degree, Scott plans on returning to the university setting to work with pre-service teachers.

Alexander Hagood graduated from Indiana University of Pennsylvania in 2015 with a bachelor of science degree in English education. After graduation, he chose to remain at IUP to continue his studies in English in the MA Composition/Literature Program, and he plans to study comparative literature at the doctoral level. Alex's academic interests include mythology and folklore, the digital humanities, and later American literature.

Caroline Lehman is in her sixth year of teaching seventh grade English language arts in the quirky land of Hershey Middle School in Hershey, Pennsylvania. Caroline has a bachelor of science degree in English Education from Indiana University of Pennsylvania and is working on a MS degree in reading from Wilkes University. Caroline has a passion for social justice and believes in the power of story to transform lives. She lives in Elizabethtown, Pennsylvania, surrounded by piles of books, and she tweets at @CarolineLehman to fangirl over YA literature, share ideas, and connect with a wider, global PLC.

Edward Litzinger is a 2015 graduate of Indiana University of Pennsylvania with a MA in teaching English. He has worked at Cambria County Child Development Corporation in Ebensburg, Pennsylvania, for five years and currently works as an alternative education teacher for troubled youth. Edward plans to continue researching and writing about the role of education in improving outcomes for students with criminal backgrounds.

Heather Lowry earned a bachelor's degree in marketing from Penn State University in 2009. She then attended Indiana University of Pennsylvania to earn a master's degree in teaching English. Since graduating from IUP in 2012, Heather has held teaching positions in different states. She is currently teaching reading at a local school district and also teaches English courses as an adjunct faculty member at a community college. In addition to teaching, Heather volunteers as a coach for the majorette squad at her alma mater high school, is actively involved with her church, and spends the majority of her free time with her friends and family. Heather hopes to continue to teach in a variety of capacities and considers herself a life-long learner. Heather lives in Indiana, Pennsylvania, with her husband and their dog Macie.

Janel Prinkey graduated from Indiana University of Pennsylvania in 2013 with a bachelor of science degree in English education. She accepted a teaching position in West Virginia, where she taught tenth and eleventh grade English before she left to pursue a master's degree in teaching reading at the University of Pittsburgh in 2015. Janel now teaches seventh and eighth grade reading in Franklin, Pennsylvania.

Sara Kirkpatrick Rhodes is a 2011 graduate of Indiana University of Pennsylvania with a bachelor of science degree in English education. While at IUP, she completed the English Honors Distinction track, as well as serving as vice-president fall 2010 and president spring 2011 of NCTE-IUP. In addition, she was selected by IUP faculty to represent IUP at the English Association of Pennsylvania State Universities annual conference held in October 2011. Since graduation, she has worked as a substitute English language arts teacher, both short- and long-term, and is currently working as a private tutor. Sara lives in Dubois, Pennsylvania, with her husband, John, and their son, Seth.

Michael Tosti is a graduate of Indiana University of Pennsylvania, having earned a bachelor of science degree in English education in 2015. Upon completing his first year of teaching, Michael began working as an editor and test developer at Vantage Laboratories. He currently works on high-stakes tests and adaptive learning pathways used in K-12 and undergraduate classrooms. In the future, Michael hopes to leverage big data and artificial technology to help teachers make informed decisions about their instruction. Michael lives with his lovely fiancée Tracy in Langhorne, Pennsylvania.

54166243R00127

Made in the USA
San Bernardino, CA
13 October 2017